THE GHOST

Twyford School at least may boast
That in it once there lived a ghost.
This ghost was very thin and tall
He had one shirt and that was all,
But of collars he had thirty,
To put one on when t'other was dirty.
On Sunday when he comes to dine
His eyes with greater lustre shine,
He cuts the cheese as if to say
I'll have some better food today.

Written by a pupil in the 1830s

TWYFORD SCHOOL

An Illustrated History

by

Roger Porteous and John Stott

Published by
George Mann Publications
Easton, Winchester,
Hampshire SO21 1ES
+44(0)1962 779944

A CIP catalogue record for this book
is available from the British Library

ISBN 9780956087478

Acknowledgements are made at the end of this book to many people who have helped with its production.

There is, however, in particular, one person without whom this project would have proved much more difficult. Charles Eglington has been a Member of the Governing Body since 1984 and has always willingly given his time and wise counsel to the School. He has unfailingly supported the authors since the inception of this book, assisting with tasks both great and small. There is an even more important reason to be grateful to him: he has most generously donated the cost of publishing this book, for which the School community owes him a considerable debt of gratitude.

George Mann Publications

Front cover: 'Boys at Play' painted in 1848 by Mr J. Hart, the drawing master.

Front endpaper: The verse, *The Ghost*, was written in the 1830s by a boy about an unpopular usher known as 'The Ghost'. The photograph, taken by Charles Dodgson in 1858, shows Mr Kitchin and Sixth form boys.

Back endpaper: Pre-Prep Children 2008.

Contents

Twyford School c1861

W.C. Benett – a pupil at Twyford until 1857 – became a civilian administrator in the United Provinces of India. The Ven. Brook Deedes, the Archdeacon of Lucknow, who had followed Benett at Twyford, said that Benett revisited the School whenever possible: it is likely that he painted this picture on one such occasion.

Foreword

It is my pleasure to introduce this book which tells the story of a school as it looks back with pride and forward with confidence. Twyford School has been on its present site for 200 years and for most of that time it has been associated with the Wickham family.

These pages tell many fascinating stories of the buildings and, most particularly, the people to whom they were so familiar – children, teachers and all those who supported them. The story of this small enduring community through the ages has been brought to life by Roger Porteous and John Stott, who have patiently researched long-forgotten archives, and have exercised the memories of those who knew the School in a different era.

There are many eminent Old Twyfordians, but there are far more unsung heroes who have lived decent lives in quiet obscurity. All of them, however, first learned at Twyford how to become good citizens and enrich the lives of those around them.

Nearly a century ago, it was fashionable to predict the demise of the prep school as an entity. Since then many have disappeared for one reason or another. Twyford has survived difficult periods, and has flourished in good times. It has had the happy knack of adapting to meet the circumstances of the day.

I think the authors have succeeded well in painting an engaging portrait of the School which has been so much a part of my life. I hope that you will enjoy this glimpse of the past as much as I have.

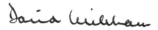

Introduction

A traveller today, journeying the short distance from the city of Winchester to the centre of the village of Twyford, might notice the tall sombre brick building bordering the road on the left, shortly before the final hill leads down to the village crossroads. Just beyond that building is a gap on the left, flanked by iron railings and brick and flint walls. That venerable entrance, lacking, as it always has done, any flamboyance, gives no clue as to the delightful vista that opens up beyond it.

Turn into this entrance: to the left, buildings of several ages range back from their centrepiece – a mellow, symmetrically styled small country house, some three hundred years old. To the right, across a well tended lawn, bordered by an historic ha-ha of unknown date, stretch green and level playing fields, framed by trees. Beyond them is the valley leading east towards Hazeley Down.

On a fine summer afternoon, with figures in white playing cricket and the unmistakable sound of tennis balls in the distance, all seems well in the world. The children wielding cricket bats and tennis rackets will be relaxing after a morning absorbing more formal elements of their education using exciting and attractively designed modern facilities undreamed of by their Latin and Greek-learning forebears – facilities largely hidden behind the older buildings that the visitor first saw on the left.

All those children from the past, were they to return today, would recognise at least some of their surroundings – the rolling landscape, the Queen Anne house, and, for many, the Chapel and Upper School. But day-to-day life for them was very different....

From an old sketch made about 1830

An earwig hunt at 'four pence per 100 caught'; a long letter home (measuring 13 feet in length – but only one and a half inches in width); the likelihood of retribution for placing 'spicula parva' (a drawing pin) on the master's chair; Captain Scott's fateful expedition to Antarctica with two sleeping bags paid for by Twyford School; the award of a Victoria Cross and 36 Military Crosses for gallantry during the South African War and the First World War – with, sadly, the loss of 80 Old Twyfordians in the latter – are all part of the deeply rooted background of the School as it enters its third century on the current site.

So too are the characters which have populated Twyford: George Marsh, the 'Mr Chips' of Twyford; Major Bull and Mr Mason, members of staff for over 50 years; and Chauce Oxenbury and Fred Stratton, who between them served 100 years as the houseman. There were others, such as Mr Grantham, the writing master, and Sergeant Alsopp, who instructed the boys in the 1850s. We catch a fleeting glimpse of them in this letter written by one of their former pupils:

> '[Mr Grantham] was a tall, thin man who seemed to be always mending quill pens, and who insisted that in writing, the pen should be in a line with the writer's shoulder…We were drilled by an old pensioner, Sgt. Alsopp, who used to walk over from Winchester in scarlet swallow-tail coat, white duck trousers and a sash. Tradition said he had been at the storming of Seringapatam [Mysore, 1799]. He spoke of the Duke of Wellington as a heathen savage might speak of his god, and his nose was suggestive of convivial habits.'

This short book attempts to give a flavour of what Twyford was like for past generations and how it has become the School that we know today.

In the Mists of the Past

The true origins of Twyford School are obscure. From at least the late seventeenth century (when the poet, Alexander Pope, is recorded as being a pupil) until 1745, there had been a Roman Catholic school at Twyford, believed to have been conducted in Segar's Buildings (Segar's). This was the name of a large house in Segar's Lane at the western end of Queen Street. The house was in existence until the last half of the twentieth century.

However, by 1745, partly as a result of passions aroused during the Jacobite Rebellions, Roman Catholicism was becoming increasingly unpopular in England and Catholic schools were in difficulty. Sometimes they were closed, occasionally they went underground and now and again they moved to a place with a more secure and confident Catholic presence. Such a place was the Benedictine college at Ware in Hertfordshire where it is known that some papers relating to a Catholic school at Twyford have been found.

What happened to the Roman Catholic school is not known. There is no clear reference to the existence of a school at Twyford during the next 48 years – except that, in the mid twentieth century, someone wrote to say that, on going through her father's library, she had come across a Latin grammar text-book labelled 'Twyford School 1775'. Sadly it never came to the School.

The next fact is that in 1793 Segar's was let by a new owner, Mr Meader, to a Mr Hannington 'for a school for the sons of Middle Class Persons'.

It is almost certain that Mr Hannington's school was not Catholic for, soon after he died towards the end of the century, Segar's Buildings and the school were sold to the vicar of Twyford, the Revd L.M. Stretch who clearly took on a going concern, without doubt already Protestant in character.

The school that was run at Segar's by Mr Hannington from 1793 can be directly traced to today's Twyford School. However, it is only if one can prove an unlikely continuity of operation between the Catholic and Protestant schools – even though we think they both used the same building – that the modern Twyford School could confidently claim seventeenth century origins.

This bookplate was designed in 1901 by Brook Kitchin, son of the earlier Headmaster, and brother of the School architect, Herbert Kitchin.

Segar's

Segar's School

Twyford Parish Magazine, February 1929 (Extract from Mr R.C. Baignent's *Registers of the Brambridge Mission in Hampshire*):

'Two miles north of Brambridge is the Village of Twyford, so well known in connection with the School maintained there from 1696 to 1745. The School is reputed to have been founded in the reign of James II, at Silkstead, of which the Rev W. Husband was the Master in 1692. This is said to have been removed in 1696 to a house at Twyford known as Segar's Buildings, formerly belonging to Anthony Segar, and sold after his death in 1693. In 1696 the School was conducted by the Rev John Banister (or Taverner).

'A vague tradition says that it was the boys at Segar's School who cheered and pursued Charles II on his way from Southampton, walking to see how the building of his new Palace at Winchester was progressing. If this was the case, it would mean that Segar's School was in existence earlier than 1696.'

Johnson's *Lives of the Poets* describes how, when Alexander Pope was about eight years old (c1696):

'He was placed in Hampshire under Taverner, a Romish priest, who by a method rarely practised, taught him the Greek and Latin rudiments together. He was now first regularly initiated in poetry by the perusal of Ogilby's Homer and Sandy's Ovid… From the care of Taverner, under whom his proficiency was considerable, he was removed to a school at Twyford, near Winchester, and to another school about Hyde Park Corner. …

'…At the last two schools he used to represent himself as having lost part of what Taverner had taught him and on his master at Twyford he had already exercised his poetry in lampoon. Yet under these masters he translated more than a fourth part of the *Metamorphoses*. If he kept the same sense of proportion to his other exercises, it cannot be thought that his loss was great…'

The Queen Anne House

In 1808, as in immediately previous years, the boys of Twyford School were being taught at the house known as Segar's. The house and the school conducted within it were still owned and run by the Vicar of Twyford, the Revd L.M. Stretch. It is believed that whilst most of the boys – for they were all boys in those days – were accommodated at Segar's, Mr Stretch had, by then, extended the vicarage to house some of them. Whether these would have been the oldest ones, or to provide more homely care for the youngest, we do not know. The vicarage was, naturally, adjacent to Twyford Church which is at the north – Winchester – end of the village.

The involvement of clergy – nearly all of them classicists themselves – in the running of small schools providing an education based on the classics, is not surprising. Such clerics were amongst the better educated people in the land. They often had available room in their rectories and vicarages, and many, having modest stipends, would have welcomed the opportunity to supplement their incomes.

We have no accurate knowledge of the total number of pupils at Mr Stretch's school or of their ages, but, as in 1815 there were 37, it is likely that the total would have been similar. Indications are that the ages would have been much as they are now, two hundred years later, in the main School – seven or eight to about 13 years – after which they went on to schools such as Winchester, Eton, Rugby or Westminster.

Whether those boys who were housed at the vicarage were taught there, or whether they had to walk to and from Segar's each day, is a matter for conjecture. Whatever the routine, it was probably inconvenient, causing the Vicar to look around for a more effective arrangement.

In, or shortly before 1808, Mr Stretch's nephew, the Revd Liscombe Clarke, had joined him as an assistant. In 1809 Mr Stretch obtained the lease of a small but elegant Queen Anne house conveniently situated near the vicarage – namely the main house at the School which we know today. He installed Mr Clarke in it straightaway.

Segar's
This picture of Segar's was painted by Dr Michael Roberts, a Twyford doctor. The building has since been demolished.

It is not known exactly when Segar's was finally vacated but, with Mr Clarke being at the present School from 1809, he would certainly have taken in the boys from the crowded vicarage at once and, doubtless, from Segar's as soon as the necessary arrangements could be made.

The Revd Stretch died in 1813 and about then Mr Clarke succeeded in converting the lease of the house to a purchase. At the same time he bought a small field, or paddock, immediately to the east.

The property leased by the Revd Stretch in 1809, and later bought outright by the Revd Clarke, was still comparatively small. The northern boundary ran east from the main road approximately along the line of the present Chapel Passage to about the south eastern corner of the modern Sports Hall. It then turned south for about 50 yards before turning westwards to the main road again. This southern boundary was roughly along the line of the ha-ha in front of the main house. It probably ended along the cob wall that still stands on the southern side of the main entrance into the School grounds. 'The Cottage' (as it became known much later) on the other side of that cob wall, was in separate ownership and was probably an old farmhouse related to the land stretching east to Bourne Lane and down towards Hazeley Road.

Now that he owned the house, Mr Clarke, needing more space, extended it northwards to the rear of the formal front part. The original house did not include anything significant beyond what is nowadays the Headmaster's Study. Mr Clarke clearly built the next section of the house as we know it – the Staff Common Room, side door and pantry areas and the rooms above them. As much of the Central Hall area is the

The Cottage

result of extensive remodelling some 80 years after his time, it is hard to recognise where Mr Clarke's work ended.

Boys at Play 1848

Mr J. Hart, Drawing Master

The small field bought with the house by the Revd Clarke became known as the Playground. It forms the foreground of the 1848 painting, 'Boys at Play', by the drawing master, Mr J. Hart, a photographic print of which is still given to every leaver. In 1989, with the levelling and reshaping of the playing fields, much of the Playground became the main car park.

The Revd Clarke was not at Twyford for long. In 1815 – the year of the Battle of Waterloo and the downfall of Napoleon – he was appointed Canon and Archdeacon of Salisbury and the School passed into the hands of the Revd James Gover Bedford. His bust stood for many years above the door into Upper School but health and safety concerns have taken their toll regarding that particular location. However, Twyfordians still pass Mr Bedford's portrait daily – it was once in the Dining Hall, but for many years has hung near the main staircase in Central Hall. There he sits, keeping a thoughtful eye on the lively successors to the children he taught and cared for.

Mr Bedford, a Scholar of Winchester and Fellow of New College, Oxford, soon felt that the site he had bought from Mr Clarke was too restricted and so he purchased a long east/west strip of land to the north. This consisted of what later became the Chapel Garden (since 2008 site of the Maths Department, but previously the Girls' Boarding Lodge) and everything to the east of that – right across to Bourne Lane. This land therefore included

The Revd J.G. Bedford ~ Headmaster 1815-1833
The boy reappeared when the picture was cleaned in the 1980s. Soot from 19th century oil lamps had gradually obscured him.

the site of the big developments of the late twentieth century, now grouped around the two courtyards.

The northern boundary of that newly purchased strip of land is thought to have been the track that formerly separated the two houses and the site of the 2008 classroom block – Saxon Court – from the main School buildings. The land to the north of this track – i.e. between the School and Bourne Lane – belonged to Twyford House (which lies on the other side of the main road). This land was to come into the School's ownership soon after the Second World War when it was bought by the School.

Appreciating what a world power the USA became during the twentieth century, it is interesting to learn that, according to one of his biographers, in the mid-eighteenth century, the great American, Benjamin Franklin, used to stroll along a fine avenue of chestnut trees that then stood on this strip of land. It was here that he discussed with his host, Bishop Jonathan Shipley, the owner of Twyford House, the growing dissatisfaction of the American colonists.

Twyford House
– framed by The Grove (the avenue of chestnuts) – sometimes known as *The Avenue*.
At the time of Franklin's visit, the main or 'high' road from Winchester to Twyford did not follow its modern course but wound down Bourne Lane *en route* to the village.

Extract from *The Life of Benjamin Franklin* by John Bigelow (1881)

'The village of Twyford lies about two miles from Winchester. Beside the old church, and close behind it, stands Twyford House, a substantial red brick dwelling of the last century, three storeys in height… The high road passes close to the house, and a little beyond the road is a fine avenue of chestnuts called the "Grove"… It was at Twyford House and whilst the guest of the "good Bishop" as Franklin habitually styled him, that he (Franklin) commenced his autobiography, and it was in the "Grove" that they used to walk for hours together discussing the crazy policy which was gradually alienating England from her choicest colonies.'

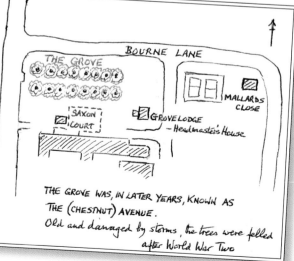

THE GROVE WAS, IN LATER YEARS, KNOWN AS THE (CHESTNUT) AVENUE.
Old and damaged by storms, the trees were felled after World War Two

Mr Bedford was Headmaster for 18 years, during which time he enlarged and improved the School's facilities considerably.

Many of the changes have, themselves, been absorbed within later alterations, but three deserve particular mention. One should imagine the square Queen Anne house as we see it today, but without other extensions or buildings to the left or right of it.

Firstly, Mr Bedford decided to build a two-storey extension on the right-hand rear corner to the east. Initially this provided a classroom on each of the two floors. The lower one is now the Boarders' Drawing Room (having been known, for many years, as Lower School). Above it was another classroom – Great Work Room – which, as we know, in due course became a dormitory.

Secondly, the Revd Bedford had taken over a school with 37 boys: by the time he left there were 50. Increasing numbers required more space. To deal with this problem he decided to use the new ground floor classroom as a dining hall and build a separate large schoolroom for teaching purposes, some distance to the east of the new extension. This new room, built in 1819 and based on the Winchester College building known as 'School', was what, from about 1860, became known as Upper School. The space between the extension and this big, new schoolroom formed a yard. Part of this contained a cloister – a covered linking passage; the rest was unroofed and used as a play area – 'Inner Court'. Later in the nineteenth century all this semi-open space was infilled with classrooms, passages and accommodation. The hard surface play area was then resited at the southern, outer end of the new schoolroom (Upper School) where, apart from a minor change in 1923, it still remains as the pitch for the ever-popular 'court cricket'.

Finally, the third interesting addition was the building, alongside the main road, of a combined brew-house, laundry and pony stable. Yes, a brew-house! Small beer – a weak brew – was the normal beverage which accompanied the boys' midday meal. Presumably, having gone through the brewing process, it was safer to drink than the water of the time. The water used for making the small beer was pumped from a nearby well by the School pony trudging around in a circle. The curved layout of the path leading today from the side door of the main house towards the Dining Hall, results directly from the site of the well which was beside it, and which is now covered with paving slabs.

The brew-house, laundry and pony stable later became the main School kitchen, above which is the Old Dining Hall.

⁂

The Cloisters, about 1856.

The School pony pumping well water
for the brewing of small beer for the boys

BEDFORD'S FIRST ADDITION

Classroom (Great Work Room)

Classroom

BEDFORD'S SECOND ADDITION — & REARRANGEMENT

Dormitory (Great Work Room)

Dining Hall   New cloister (passage) alongside an open area known as Inner Court

Large Schoolroom (in which all the boys were taught)

In the above figurative drawing, the Dining Hall was later to become, at various times, a classroom (known as 'Lower School'), the Library and, latterly, the Boarders' Drawing Room.

The kitchen which served this Dining Hall was sited in what in later years became the Matron's Room Lobby.

This large Schoolroom, built in 1819, was, in due course, to be called 'Upper School'. Later still, the area of the cloister and Inner Court would be infilled with, firstly, a gymnasium, and then classrooms and accommodation for both staff and boys. Inner Court was, as a result, resited as an open play area on the outer end of Upper School.

Inner Court and the covered cloister,
looking towards the Dining Hall

The Schoolroom (later known as Upper School)
looking north. The stage was added later.

The glimpses of life at Twyford in the Revd Bedford's time, as seen in the archives, are few in number, but they are most evocative of the period.

There is a slim book containing the complete School lists of 'The Names of Young Gentlemen educated at Twyford' for each of the 37 'half years' of Mr Bedford's headship. Each list is in the same elegant copperplate handwriting – Mr Bedford's? Included within that book is the boys' clothing list which includes '4 Night Shirts and 4 Night Caps' together with '3 Suits of Clothes (2 for little Boys)'.

Mr Mark Lowth (Old Twyfordian), who was Chairman of Twyford School Trust for some years at the end of the twentieth century, has made available to us two short, beautifully written, rather formal letters posted home by an ancestor – Charles Lowth – in 1817 and 1818. The standards of writing taught and achieved by, probably, most of the boys, were exceptionally high by later standards. A contemporary of Charles Lowth was Richard Chenevix Trench who later became Archbishop of Dublin and in 1858 provided the inspiration for the creation of the New Oxford English Dictionary. Another schoolmate was Thomas Garnier, who was to become Dean of Lincoln.

© Representative Church Body

Richard Chenevix Trench (1807–1886)
Chenevix Trench attended Twyford (1816-1819) and subsequently became a priest and scholar. He served in parishes near Twyford, and later became Dean of Westminster, and Archbishop of Dublin during the turbulent period of the disestablishment of the Church of Ireland. He was buried in Westminster Abbey.

Thomas Garnier (1809-1863)

He was the second son of Dean Garnier (1776-1873) of Winchester. Records show a 'Garnier, T.' joining the School in 1817. Garnier went on to Winchester, and subsequently rowed for Oxford in the first boat race against Cambridge, at Henley in 1829. He also played cricket, together with his brother, for the University against MCC.

He was ordained and later in life served as Dean of Ripon (briefly, as he found the accommodation inadequate) and then as Dean of Lincoln.

In addition to saving souls, Garnier once saved a lady from incineration. He was at a party, conversing by the fireside with the Marchioness of Blandford. Suddenly her crinoline dress caught fire. Garnier threw her to the floor and wrapped her in the hearthrug to save her from the flames.

Garnier and his wife had seven sons and seven daughters. One of them was Keppel Garnier who was at Twyford from 1855 to 1859 and whose photograph appears on page 26.

(opposite) **The first School List and Clothes List, 1815**
Annual lists of boys were entered in this book by the Revd J.G. Bedford, Headmaster 1815-1833. There were 37 boys in 1815; by 1833 the number had risen to 50. The clothes list records the standard items of clothing each boy was required to bring with him to the School.

List of BOYS at the REV? J. G. BEDFORD's from August 1815 to Christmas 1815.

Alves

Alves

Alves

Aldridge

Bussell

Bostobetter

Blair

Beckley

Colt

Courtenay

Cox

Carnegie

Everett

Fooks

Grant

Grant

Hulton

Heathcote

Hamilton

Hamilton

Hay

Litchfield

Lowth

Lowth

Prevost

Phillips

Rawlinson

Shedden

Shedden

Shum

Stewart

Swinton

Winterbottom

Wither

Wither

Wools

Wickham

The usual List of Linen &c. brought by each Boy to the Rev? James Gower Bedford's.

6 Shirts.

4 Night Shirts

4 Night Caps.

8 Pair of Cotton Stockings.

6 Pair of Worsted Stockings.

3 Suits of Clothes. (2 for little Boys)

2 Hats. 1 Great Coat.

8 Pocket Handkerchiefs.

6 Pin Cloths.

3 Pair of Shoes.

6 Linen Towels.

Combs, Brushes. &c.

N. B. It is requested that all Linen and other articles of Dress may be marked with the name at full length.

Summer Clothes if convenient.

A fresh and correct Inventory must be sent every half year.

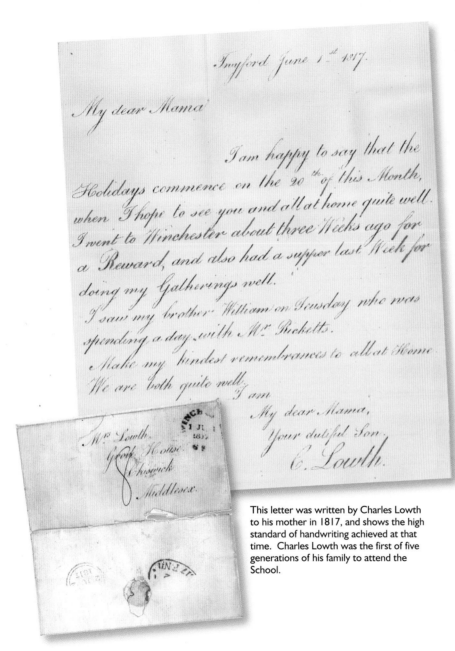

Twyford June 1st 1817.

My dear Mama

I am happy to say that the Holidays commence on the 20th of this Month, when I hope to see you and all at home quite well. I went to Winchester about three Weeks ago for a Reward, and also had a supper last Week for doing my Gatherings well.

I saw my brother William on Tuesday who was spending a day with Mr. Ricketts.

Make my kindest remembrances to all at Home We are both quite well.

I am My dear Mama, Your dutiful Son.

C. Lowth.

This letter was written by Charles Lowth to his mother in 1817, and shows the high standard of handwriting achieved at that time. Charles Lowth was the first of five generations of his family to attend the School.

Frederick Bell Pryor (1822-1860)

For well over 100 years Frederick Bell Pryor has kept an eye on the passing generations of children, and they will have glanced occasionally at him. But who was he, and what became of him?

Frederick Bell Pryor came to Twyford when he was eight years old, about the time the portrait was painted. He was a pupil of the Revd Bedford from 1830-1833.

His father kept a diary, and this entry describes young Fred's first day at Twyford:

October 9, 1830: 'Proceeded to Twyford in a post chaise at 12 o'clock, three miles from Winchester, found Mr. and Mrs. Bedford at home expecting us. We went over the whole establishment, which gave both my wife and myself great satisfaction. Mr. Bedford himself is blind, but a very superior man. There are four masters besides in the School and Mrs. Bedford is a most intelligent and active lady. There are 50 boys and it requires two or three years to get admission. We left dear Fred very comfortable.'

After Twyford Fred went to Winchester and Oxford, where he was a Fellow of New College for some years. He got heavily into debt whilst at Oxford, as did many students, and was pressed into ordination by his father. He married in 1849, and two years later became Rector of Benington, Hertfordshire, a living of which his father, a brewer, was patron. He spent the last nine years of his life there, and died in 1860 aged 38.

His portrait was presented to the School in 1901 by his daughter, Mrs Shirley, by which date at least 11 members of their family had been Twyfordians.

Bedford's Slate

There is a small wood-framed slate fixed to the wall at the doorway from Upper School into the Library, where it has been for as long as anyone can remember. On it are the three words *inepti, tardi* and *inurbani*. It was suggested by Bob Wickham in his book *Shades of the Prison House*, that the slate was instituted by the Revd Bedford. Boys whose names were listed too frequently on the slate had an appointment with the Headmaster: corporal punishment was a standard form of chastisement then and for many subsequent years. The canes were kept in a cupboard behind the panelling close to the slate.

There is little doubt, says Bob Wickham, that most headmasters of Mr Bedford's time 'were almost criminally negligent of what went on outside the classrooms, and physical conditions in all schools were primitive beyond description'.

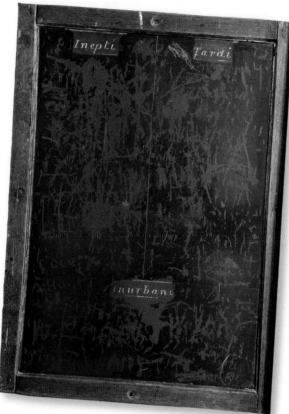

This slate can still be seen on the frame of the Memorial Library door.

CRIME...

inepti: names of boys whose work was careless or shoddy

tardi: those who were late

inurbani: here were listed the bad-mannered or ill-behaved

...and PUNISHMENT

The penalty for too many appearances on the 'slate'

Nevertheless, many boys seemed to have looked on their schooldays with pleasure! The fact that Twyford's numbers had expanded during Mr Bedford's time shows that the School that he ran was by no means unpopular. Most importantly, he had taken on to his staff a graduate of Christ Church, Oxford, the first Revd Robert Wickham. This appointment, in the early nineteenth century, was to lead to the remarkable and invaluable connection of the Wickham family as owners and/or headmasters – often both at the same time – that lasted until the retirement of Mr David Wickham as Headmaster in 1983. However, Mr Bedford, with Mr Wickham as an assistant master, still had several years of headship ahead of him.

In due course, with his eyesight failing, Mr Bedford decided to retire: at the end of 1833 he sold the School to his assistant, the Revd Robert Wickham.

As we have seen, Mr Wickham, then only 31 years of age, had already taught at Twyford for some time and the change in headship probably  made little immediate difference to the daily lives of the boys. However, he was to be Headmaster for 13 years and some alterations and additions were to be expected as time went by.

Firstly, though, what was school life like in 1834? What did the boys learn? How was the year organised?

A feature of the age was teaching by catechisms – questions and answers.

The Revd Robert Wickham
Headmaster 1834-1848

This form of teaching appealed to Bedford to the extent that he wrote and published in about 1840 a book entitled *Questions for Junior Classes*, which was used at Twyford for many years. It was divided into numerous sections on obscure subjects which ranged from Kings of Israel and Signs of the Zodiac to the seven birthplaces of Homer and rhetorical prosopopoeia.

In addition to catechisms, a heavily classical curriculum with a great deal of learning by rote was also a typical feature of education in the mid nineteenth century. At Twyford it was normal for the senior boys to recite up to 600 lines of Latin or Greek prose or verse at one time. For the award of a prize, considerably more was expected. Such a prize was won in 1833 by Thomas Hughes – the future author and Queen's Counsel – for narrating 1,200 lines that he had learnt by heart: he was ten years old.

Although the railway system was beginning to spread, transport to and from many parts of the country was still slow and far from easy. As a result the School year continued to be divided into two halves, each separated from the other by about six weeks holiday around Christmas and in the summer. Five days off at Easter for local boys was the only other break in the year. Exeats were not even a twinkle in a soothsayer's eye – let alone the eye of a new headmaster.

Changes in the School itself included the provision of improved washing facilities (which were probably not fully appreciated by the 'young gentlemen'), and the reversal in the order of the courses at the boys' dinners, from 'pudding (usually suet) before meat' to the arrangement with which we are now familiar. Suet had been more expensive than meat but this was changing and meat became the higher status food. Meals were taken in wearisome silence, but reading was allowed.

Of greater significance to those who came to Twyford in later years was Mr Wickham's acquisition of land. He obtained possession of the fields south of the School, down to the Hazeley Road, and he leased The Cottage (beside the main entrance) and the land south of it, bordering the Winchester road: this provided the site for the eventual building of the large house called Serle's Hill – nowadays the core of the Pre-Prep. In due course all the leased property came into the actual ownership of Robert Wickham himself or his descendents, and a great deal of that was transferred to the ownership of the newly formed Twyford School Trust in 1956.

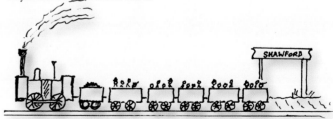

© Watts Gallery

Thomas Hughes, best known as the author of the semi-autobiographical public school classic, *Tom Brown's Schooldays* (1857), arrived at Twyford in 1830, aged eight. Subsequently, the boys who were at Twyford when *Tom Brown's Schooldays* was published were very proud of him, and 'Tom Brown' was painted on the dormitory bed he had occupied.

The portrait shown here, painted by G.F. Watts, appeared in the first edition of *Tom Brown's Schooldays*.

School rules written by Thomas Hughes

'Let all be silent all finish there meals without lounging wastefulness or greediness. Let decency be observed at the grace and order in entering and leaving the hall. Let morning and evening prayer be invariably said by the bed side let all be obedient to the upper servant and school nurse and the juniors to the seniors of their room conversation is permitted but no loud speaking or play cleanliness and good manners are enjoined 8 minutes are allowed before the morning bell and fifteen minutes more in the washing room. Let each boy show himself to the nurse according to his number and directions and at all times let him apply to the school nurse before he shall be allowed to appear in the parlour.'

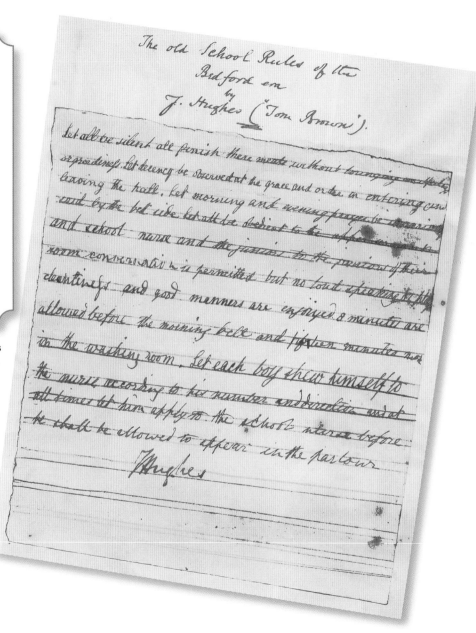

A Twyford Letter

This transcript of a letter shown below, written in 1840, gives an admirable example of early marketing.

It had been sent by the Third Master of the School – James Roberts – to a Mr Hughes, in response to an enquiry about the suitability of Twyford for Mr Hughes' son, Hugh, who – it was hoped – would successfully go on to Eton. It seems that James Roberts' father was an acquaintance or friend of Mr Hughes and had suggested Twyford for his son.

The middle part of this letter (omitted here) is a fairly detailed breakdown of the various Ancient Greek and Latin texts studied by the boys in each of the four year groups into which the School was then divided.

The Mr Wickham referred to in the letter is, of course, the Revd Robert Wickham who was clearly running a successful school in that the numbers are said by Roberts, in his letter, usually to be higher than Mr Wickham's target number of 50.

It probably helped that the Second Master's learning was 'only equalled by his amiability and unaffected piety'!

TWYFORD
WINTON
October 24, 1840

'My dear sir,

I am desired to write and give you a description of Twyford and its system – the boys, their ages, number and character – for my father seems to think that you would be glad to know all particulars, as you have not yet satisfied yourself as to where you will fix Hugh before he goes to Eton. It is our business to prepare boys for this school, as much as for any other: indeed, the greater number of late have proceeded thither. Mr. Wickham's

number is 50 but we generally count some fifty-six or seven. It is essentially a preparatory school and intended for young children: in the junior class their ages vary from 7 to 10 and I don't think there is a boy at the top of the school who can yet number thirteen years. We could not keep them here after 14…

'… one of Mr. Wickham's first principles [is] to discountenance and indeed to forbid fagging or any thing approaching to it, venerable and time honoured though it be. Senior boys are taught to consider their juniors as under their protection and I have every reason to believe that this feeling prevails generally throughout the school. As for the "larning", you may be interested to know that there are 4 classes…Throughout the whole school grammar and prosody are the staple commodities…The holidays are seven weeks at Christmas and as many at midsummer and though last not least, the terms are £80 and this I believe covers nearly all expenses...

'Mr. Wickham takes a most active part both as manager and teacher, in both of which characters I think him unsurpassed by all the world beside: I have certainly never met with or heard of anyone like him. He is remarkable for those three things which someone has pronounced to be characteristics of a wise and good man: he never loses his temper, he rules his household well and he writes a letter without needless repetition...

'The second master is a clergyman who took high honours at Cambridge, and whose learning is only equalled by his amiability and unaffected piety. You will think I am "laying it on thick" in all quarters but I am afraid I must stop here and content myself with saying that the third master desires his very best regards [be sent] to Mrs. Hughes and remains

Your faithful servant
JAMES C. ROBERTS.

'We are within three hours distance of London. If there is any other point which you desire to have explained I shall be very happy to tell you all I can about it.'

The Oldest Prep School?

Towards the end of the nineteenth century, controversy arose between rival claimants 'to be the oldest Preparatory School'. A factor in this discussion was the upper age of the boys in these schools. Twyford's Headmaster became interested and wrote to several elderly gentlemen who had been at the School in Bedford's day (1815-1833) to find out the ages at which boys left. One of the replies, from the Revd G.W. Paul, who left Twyford four years before the start of Queen Victoria's reign, and written a few days after she died, is shown to the right:

'From the Revd G.W. Paul

Jan 28th 1901

'Dear Mr Wickham

I left Twyford School in 1833, and my impression is that there were no boys in the school at that time above the age of 13 or 14. I went to Twyford in 1830, and well remember that the head boy at that time was Farrer, either the late Lord Farrer or his brother. Tom Hughes and his brother were my contemporaries, and also two of the Arnolds. I fear that at my age I shall never visit the dear old haunts again, but they ever live in my remembrance.
Yours very truly
G.W. Paul'

Tom Brown's Schooldays

Thomas Hughes left Twyford for Rugby in 1833. The early sequences of his famous novel were set at Twyford, and the following description evokes those days:

'These half-holiday walks were the great events of the week. The whole fifty boys started after dinner with one of the ushers for Hazeldown, which was distant some mile or so from the school. Hazeldown measured some three miles round, and in the neighbourhood were several woods full of all manner of birds and butterflies. The usher walked slowly round the down with such boys as liked to accompany him; the rest scattered in all directions, being only bound to appear again when the usher had completed his round, and accompany him home. They were forbidden however to go anywhere except on the down and into the woods; the village being especially prohibited, where huge bulls'-eyes and unctuous toffy might be procured in exchange for coin of the realm.

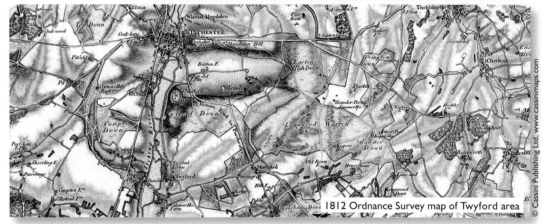

1812 Ordnance Survey map of Twyford area

© Cassini Publishing Ltd, www.cassinimaps.com

'Various were the amusements to which the boys then betook themselves. At the entrance of the down there was a steep hillock, like the barrows of Tom's own downs. This mound was the weekly scene of terrific combats, at a game called by the queer name of "mud-patties". The boys who played divided into sides under different leaders, and one side occupied the mound. Then, all parties having provided themselves with many sods of turf, cut with their bread-and-cheese knives, the side which remained at the bottom proceeded to assault the mound, advancing up on all sides under cover of a heavy fire of turfs, and then struggling for victory with the occupants, which was theirs as soon as they could, even for a moment, clear the summit, when they in turn became the besieged. It was a good rough dirty game, and of great use in counteracting the sneaking tendencies of the school.'

Although still comparatively young, the Revd Robert Wickham was persuaded, for family reasons, to give up the headship in 1848 and become the Archdeacon of St Asaph in North Wales. He retained ownership of the School but appointed the Revd J.C. Roberts to be Headmaster. Mr Roberts had risen to the level of Second Master and had been in that post for some time. He remained at Twyford for only six years during which time we know of no changes or additions. By 1854 it was clear that the School was not as successful as it had been and Roberts retired to become incumbent of a parish.

Looking southwards towards Hampshire, Robert Wickham must have been most concerned about the school that he owned but had left in another's hands. He probably then contacted his old College authorities at Oxford to seek advice. Whether or not he did, a brilliant young University Tutor at Christ Church, still only 28 years of age, decided to assume the headship at Twyford. He took over a school with under 40 boys and left it seven years later, with 74. The School was to be transformed. The new Headmaster was the Revd George William Kitchin, later in life to become not only a distinguished academic at Oxford, but also Dean of Winchester and, in due course, Dean of Durham and first Chancellor of Durham University. How was this transformation achieved?

Although the curriculum – an excerpt from which is shown opposite – remained much as in Bedford's time, and discipline severe and even cruel by modern standards, the relationship between Kitchin and his pupils was far more humane than was the norm for the day. He expected the teaching by his staff to be stimulating as well as informative and he involved himself with the boys' pursuits and hobbies. He was interested in all kinds of natural phenomena, in music and light-hearted theatricals.

He led rambling and climbing expeditions and, almost unbelievably for his era, worked with a team of boys in digging out the foundations of a long cloister that later became the Chapel Passage.

Kitchin was constructing this cloister (a covered arcade) to link the main school building to Bedford's combined brew-house, laundry and stable which stood beside the main

The Revd G.W. Kitchin
photographed by his friend Charles Dodgson

road. He was converting that building into the one that we use today – the kitchen on the ground floor and, above it, what we call the Old Dining Hall. Kitchin, initially, intended this upper room to be a schoolroom and almost immediately after its completion held a School concert in it: amongst the five adults and nine boys who performed was a young Hubert Parry, who had only recently arrived at the School. The cloister would provide rain-proof access to this new room which from 1860 would be used as the School's Dining Hall.

ζῷον, — living thing.
ἱμάτιον, — garment.
κέντρον, — goad, spur.
μέτρον, — measure.
ὅπλον, — armour (of def
πεδίον, — plain.
πρόσωπον, — face.
σημεῖον, — sign.
στρατόπεδον, — camp.
τόξον, — bow.
τροπαῖον, — trophy.
χωρίον, — place, spot.

Like νοῦς (for νόος), m
ἀδελφιδοῦς (for εο·ς), nephe

THIRD DECLENSION.

Soft-Vowel Stem

Like πόλις, mostly

αἴσθησις, ἡ, — perc
ἀνάβασις, ἡ, — goin
δύναμις, ἡ, — pow
ἕξις, ἡ, — hab
κρίσις, ἡ, — jud
λύσις, ἡ, — rele
μάθησις, ἡ, — lea
μάντις, ὁ, — soo
ὄφις, ὁ, — sn
ὄψις, ἡ, — si
πίστις, ἡ, — t
πρᾶξις, ἡ, — d
πρόφασις, ἡ,
στάσις, ἡ,
τάξις, ἡ,
τέρψις, ἡ,
φύσις, ἡ,

Like οὖς, mu

ἄρκυς, ἡ,
βότρυς, ὁ,
γένυς, ἡ,
δρῦς, ἡ,

Timetable or 'Table of Hours' for a typical day in April 1856		
Monday	Upper Division	Lower Division
7.00 – 7.45	Learn Xenophon	Learn Homer
9.15 – 10.00	Say Xenophon	Say Homer
10.05 – 11.00	1st Verse Task	1st Verse Task
11.30 – 12.30	French	French
12.30 – 1.00	Nicholl's Help	Nicholl's Help
3.30 – 4.30	Music and Drawing	Music or Drawing
4.45 – 5.45	Mathematics	Mathematics
7.00 – 7.45	Greek Grammar	Greek Grammar

Mr Kitchin and Boys 1858
Mr Hart, the Drawing Master, is on the right.
The picture was taken by Charles Dodgson.

As if this 'Table of Hours' was not daunting enough, there was, at the end of each term, a 'Standing-Up' when every boy was required to recite some pieces which he had learned by heart – the senior boys being expected to offer 500-600 lines, whereas the IV Form only had to narrate 325-400 lines.

A single verse of a psalm represented one line, worth one mark to the VI Form but probably two marks in the IV Form.

Shown here is an extract from a typical set of passages which could be chosen by a boy in the VI Form, with the weighting in lines and marks that each would carry.

VI Form: maximum to be offered 600 lines, minimum 500 lines.

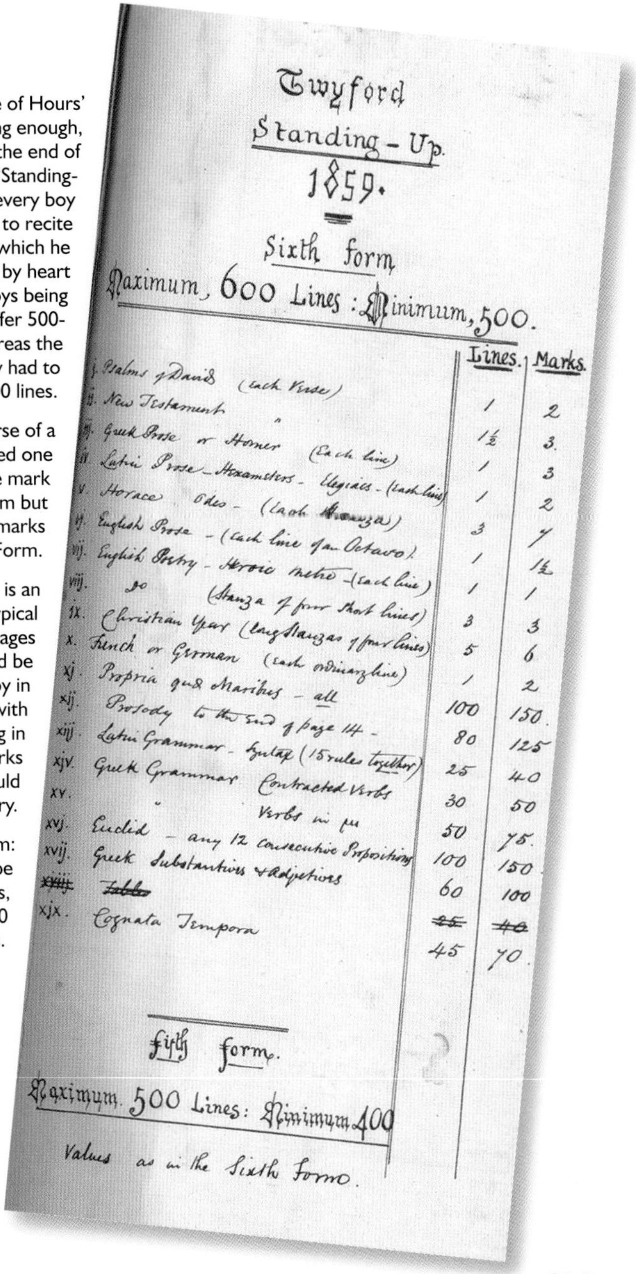

Twyford
Standing-Up.
1859.

Sixth Form
Maximum, 600 Lines: Minimum, 500.

		Lines	Marks
i.	Psalms of David (each Verse)	1	2
ii.	New Testament "	1½	3
iii.	Greek Prose or Homer (Each line)	1	3
iv.	Latin Prose – Hexameters. Elegiacs. (Each line)	1	3
v.	Horace Odes – (Each Stanza)	3	2
vi.	English Prose – (Each line of an Octavo)	3	4
vii.	English Poetry – Heroic metre (each line)	1	1½
viii.	do (Stanza of four short lines)	1	1
ix.	Christian Year (long Stanzas of four lines)	3	3
x.	French or German (each ordinary line)	5	6
xi.	Propria quæ Maribus – all	1	2
xii.	Prosody to the end of page 14	100	150
xiii.	Latin Grammar – Syntax (15 rules together)	80	125
xiv.	Greek Grammar Contracted Verbs	25	40
xv.	" Verbs in μι	30	50
xvi.	Euclid – any 12 consecutive Propositions	50	75
xvii.	Greek Substantives & adjectives	100	150
xviii.	Tables	60	100
xix.	Cognata Tempora	45	70

Fifth Form.
Maximum, 500 Lines: Minimum, 400.
Values as in the Sixth Form.

The Revd Kitchin's short headship was notable in several ways: two of these remain part of our lives today, namely the number of terms in a year and organised sports with matches against other schools.

The railway system had improved vastly during recent years, making travelling between a child's home and his boarding school far more practicable than it had been. As a result, the short Easter break of five days previously enjoyed only by local boys, was extended to make the sort of holiday to which we are accustomed. Now pupils could travel home more easily wherever they lived. The three terms per year pattern had arrived. What a relief that must have been for those young boys to whom a 20-week term, under the austere disciplinary, academic and living conditions of the day, would have seemed terribly daunting. The teachers were probably just as thankful – as in their case they would have more frequent rests from hearing endless recitations of Xenophon and Virgil in halting Ancient Greek or Latin.

Although by Kitchin's time, organised games were becoming well established in the public schools, preparatory schools were generally too small to undertake much sport other than rudimentary games of football on a playground. However, Kitchin began to do better than that, for he has left us a photograph – still a comparatively new technique – showing what must have been a formal game of cricket with well tended grass and players in white. What is more, in 1858, a delightful report was published in the *Hampshire Chronicle*, describing a cricket match played at Shawford House: 'The Juniors of Eton College v The Twyford School'. A second match was played that term against a junior team of Wykehamists.

Kitchin was also an enthusiastic swimmer with the result that most of the 60 or so boys learned to swim in the nearby River Itchen, as they were still doing half a century later when the new Swimming Bath was built.

Hubert Parry

These boys, Guise and Parry (*right*), would have known the rigours of the 'Table of Hours' and 'Standing Up' well. Hubert Parry was born in 1848 and came to Twyford when he was ten. He was probably fortunate in that he was at the School during G.W. Kitchin's headship, for music was one of

A. Guise and C.H.H. Parry 1860

the many extra-curricular activities actively encouraged by this inspirational man. Parry and the young Charles Wickham, the future Headmaster, were contemporaries. They had their first music lesson together and sang duets in School concerts.

Parry went on to Eton and Oxford and, when only 35 years of age, was appointed a professor at the Royal College of Music. He became one of England's most notable composers, writing many works. Today, his most well known piece of music is arguably his setting of William Blake's poem *Jerusalem*. He also composed the tune (later named *Repton*) to which the hymn *Dear Lord and Father of Mankind* is most often sung.

1858.
The Twyford Eleven

VV. Marshall C. Malet Grant R. Stiphinson J. Frederick Duthy Lawrence Richardson R. Clutton Duncombe J. Clutton

Cricket 1858
The porch of the
School can be seen on
the far right.

Almost
130
years
after this
match the old
Mound Stand
at Lord's was
being modernised
and the School
bought several of the
redundant but elegant
benches.

ETON, WINTON, AND RUGBY.

First innings.			Second innings.	
A. Ricardo, b C. Malet		6	st J. Hart, b C. Malet	0
S. Malet, run out		2	c J. Clutton, b C. Malet	11
T. Chamberlayne, c R. Stephenson, b C. Malet		0	c J. Hart, J. Frederick	1
W. Long, st J. Hart, b C. Malet		2	c J. Hart, b C. Malet	2
H. Stewart, c Duncombe, b C. Malet		15	run out	32
J. Long, run out		5	b Stephenson	22
— Ravenhall, run out		0	b J. Frederic	12
C. Frederic, b C. Malet		3	b C. Malet	1
— Heathcote, c Darby, b C. Malet		0	not out	0
— Malet		2	c F. Richardson, b C. Malet	0
Turner, not out		0		4
Byes		1	byes	1
Leg byes		3	leg byes	14
Wide balls		0	wide balls	2
No balls			no balls	
		38		102

TWYFORD SCHOOL.

C. Duncombe, run out		4	b W. Long	1
J. Clutton, b A. Ricardo		7	b C. Frederick	4
J. Hart, c Turner, b A. Ricardo		5	st Stewart, b Ricardo	8
R. Stephenson, run out		0	c and b Chamberlayne	0
J. Frederick, b Chamberlayne		0	b Chamberlayne	0
W. Marshall, not out		5	c Turner, b Chamberlayne	0
C. Malet, l b w, b Chamberlayne		0	b Chamberlayne	5
A. Duthy, l b w, b Chamberlayne		0	not out	0
J. Dillon, b Chamberlayne		0	b C. Frederick	3
W. Darby, b Chamberlayne		0	run out	1
Byes		1	byes	8
Wide balls		0	wide balls	1
No balls		0	no balls	
		22		44

THE JUNIORS OF ETON COLLEGE v. THE TWYFORD SCHOOL.

Perhaps at no period of its history was the fine, open-air, noble game more generally patronised or better played than at the present time; and of the numberless matches played in all parts of the country, none more keenly contested, nor looked to with a wider interest than those known as the "public games," the Wykehamites having this season won the annual game with the Etonians.

On Wednesday the junior eleven of Eton college met the eleven of the Twyford school at Shawford-house, the seat of General Frederic. Though the school was given one of the masters, who is a player, yet, from the advanced age of the Etonians, it was expected to be an uphill game. The wickets were fixed on the lawn at half-past ten, and the game commenced shortly after by Eton going to the wickets to face the bowling of J. Frederic and Malet, and from the commencement to the close the game was played beautifully; old and practised hands looking on expressed unfeigned admiration at the steady precision and finished style of the players.

The bowling of John St. John Frederic, a handsome curly-wigged lad of 14, was so sharp, that the fielding was almost entirely behind the wicket. C. Malet's bowling was greatly admired.

The fielding was capital. The few chances offered were taken without mistake, three good catches being made by R. Stephenson, C. Duncombe, and W. Darby; and in the second innings two by F. Richardson and a long catch by J. Clutton.

Stewart, of the Winchester College, kept the wicket for Eton with the ease and grace that distinguishes him; J. Hart kept the wicket well for Twyford.

By the afternoon the grounds became very animated. In the centre of the lawn the game, every ball increasing in interest—the pastime approved by the presence of the esteemed principal of the school and other clergy—ladies and gentlemen of the neighbouring families—the fifty or sixty scholars of the school—groups of collegians from Winchester—nor were the villagers denied—all backed by the fine old mansion and lofty luxuriant woods, contributed to make a hearty and thoroughly English scene.

The hospitalities were rich and abundant, and presided over by a solicitude for the happiness of all, that appeared to be perfectly successful. The shades of evening closed upon a delightfully passed day, and it may be doubted if the cheers and gratulations that greeted the ear of "Good Queen Bess," who was feasted at this hall, were louder—certainly not more sincere—than those that "woke the echoes" on this occasion, in grateful acknowledgements to the general and his amiable lady.

Source: Hampshire Chronicle, 1858

23

The unusual records left by the Revd Kitchin – now in the archives – are his Black Book and his great scrapbook.

The Black Book is only 7½ inches by 5 inches by 1 inch thick but it is most intriguing. It was really an extension of Bedford's 'slate'. In the Black Book Kitchin lists the names of boys who have committed serious offences, together with, on occasions, the punishments awarded – but all in Latin: for example, a beating is shown as 'capitis damnatus'. Perhaps the most amusing entry, translated from its Latin, is 'Hill: ill-behaved in that he fixed a small pin on the chair of the third master so that the third master was all but seriously wounded. Condemned to punishment.' Kitchin's humanity shows yet again, however, as, in order to balance the Black Book, he introduced a system of Good Conduct Prizes. In 1857, out of a school of 50 boys, 16 were awarded such prizes. The carrot and stick approach, together with more interesting and enlightened teaching, was working for in that same year two scholarships and two exhibitions to Winchester were awarded.

The great scrapbook, which must have taken Kitchin countless hours to compile, is a remarkable record of the School's organisation and curriculum.

A final but interesting point to make about Kitchin is his close friendship with Charles Dodgson, alias Lewis Carroll, author of *Alice in Wonderland*. The connections are hard to disentangle! Kitchin had come from an academic post at Christ Church, Oxford where Charles Dodgson had become a Mathematics tutor in 1855. The Dean of Christ Church was, from 1855, Henry Liddell (the father of Alice upon whom Dodgson modelled his famous character); the Liddell and Dodgson boys were 'sent to Kitchin at Twyford' (Alice's younger brother certainly being one of these). Charles Dodgson was a keen photographer and took many photographs of pupils and staff during his visits to Twyford. Many

of these are in Kitchin's scrapbook, as are some by Reginald Southey, another well-known photographer.

When at the end of 1861 Kitchin returned to Oxford – still only 35 years old – he left behind a school that was successful and beginning to adapt to a changing educational world. It was a time of enquiry and endeavour. During Kitchin's few years at Twyford, Charles Darwin was writing his great work, *On the Origin of Species* (published in 1859), and Dr David Livingstone was struggling to open up central Africa to trade – and coming across the wonderful Victoria Falls of the Zambezi in the process. Kitchin's interest in all kinds of natural phenomena, shared with the boys by means of scientific lectures by visitors such as the local doctor, had therefore been very much in the spirit of the age.

Kitchin's successor was to be the Revd Latham Wickham who had been born at Twyford where his father, Robert, had recently become Headmaster in succession to Bedford. Latham Wickham had worked under Kitchin at Twyford for the previous eighteen months so presumably had been influenced by Kitchin's style and ethos.

The Mulberry Tree
Silkworms were kept on the tree
during the Second World War

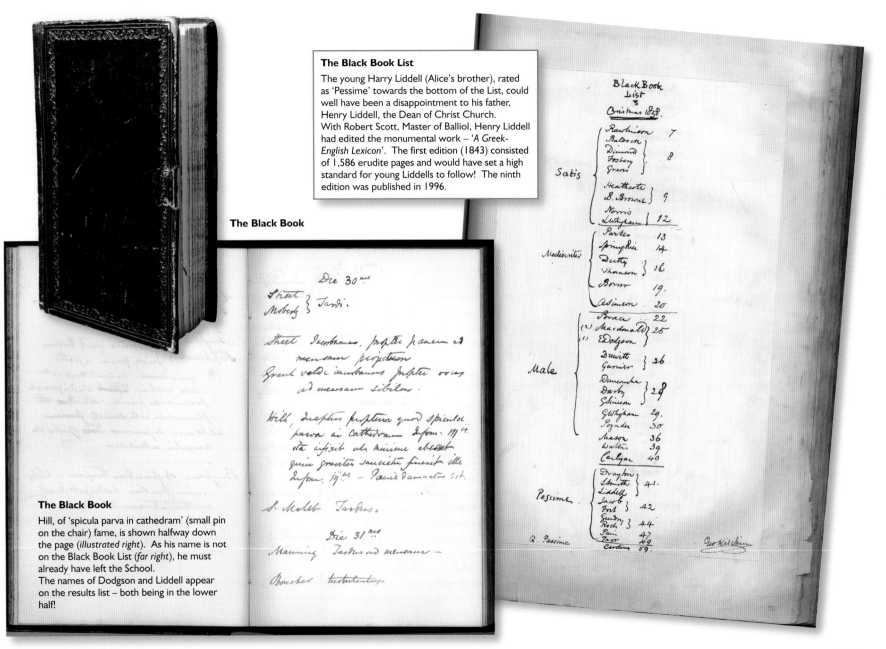

The Black Book

The Black Book List

The young Harry Liddell (Alice's brother), rated as 'Pessime' towards the bottom of the List, could well have been a disappointment to his father, Henry Liddell, the Dean of Christ Church. With Robert Scott, Master of Balliol, Henry Liddell had edited the monumental work – '*A Greek-English Lexicon*'. The first edition (1843) consisted of 1,586 erudite pages and would have set a high standard for young Liddells to follow! The ninth edition was published in 1996.

The Black Book

Hill, of 'spicula parva in cathedram' (small pin on the chair) fame, is shown halfway down the page (*illustrated right*). As his name is not on the Black Book List (*far right*), he must already have left the School.

The names of Dodgson and Liddell appear on the results list – both being in the lower half!

25 ✧

Mids 1858
The Sixth Form

G.W.K. Richardson: Dicken: W.Marshall: Manning: Deedes: Dalby: Lawrence: J.Clutton: R.Clutton.
3. 1. 4. 2. 6. 5. 9. 8. 7.

This photograph was taken by Charles Dodgson in 1858

The 'Measles' Register
Such illnesses were a scourge
of 19th century school life

Keppel Garnier

Keppel Garnier was a grandson of Dean Garnier (1776-1873) of Winchester, and a son of Dean Garnier (1809-1863) of Lincoln. Despite his well-scrubbed appearance and eminent forebears, he was a fairly average schoolboy. At Twyford between 1855 and 1859, he was bottom of Form 1 in December 1858. He was also listed under 'male' (bad) in the Black Book for that month (*see page 25*). Having only one black mark more (at 26) than E. Dodgson, Garnier was not as bad as Alice Liddell's brother who had accumulated 41 such marks and was rated 'pessime' (worst!). Keppel Garnier joined the Royal Navy, was promoted Sub Lieutenant in 1867, and by 1891 had retired as a Commander.

1 Oct.ber 1857

My dear mama
I rally do not kown what to say. I hope you are quite well. We have had verey fine weteaher. ~~delet~~ I must be called a Micllmus ~~gous~~ by whom I banhan tell you. I'ts verey stupid to be write'ing here dall the time. with nothing to say, and somebody I kown want. tell me what to say. We had tea ~~#~~ out

Extract from R. Faber's first monthly letter home. How one can sympathise with the little chap!

An early method of pest control

By Proclamation   June 24. 1859.

Earwigs, dead or alive, at 1d. per Hundredhead.

Deedes & Co	3725
Richardson	1275
Fosbery & Co	950
Mazow & Milbanke	925
Phipps & Unwin	850
G Whigham	650
Chalet & Duncombe	450
C. Kildin & Co	350
Drewitt	275
Maden & H Phipps	225
Poynder	200
Macdonald Bel & Co	175
A Simeon	150
Brace	75
Yarton & Co	50
Lindoes	50
	10,375

Young Philip Lindoe really shows promise…

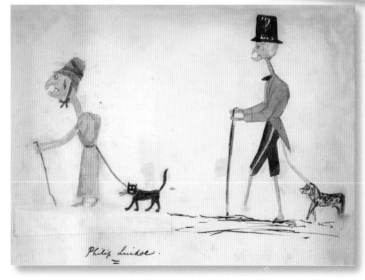

Philip Lindoe.

Whilst learning a little about life at the School in earlier days, it can be interesting to see it in a broader context. For instance, what would the Headmaster of the day have been reading about in his copy of *The Times*?

It was during Kitchin's years at Twyford that war artists and correspondents began to follow military campaigns in person. As a result the reports in the press benefited from greater accuracy and immediacy than before.

Kitchin's first experience of this would have been William Russell's startling reports in *The Times*, firstly of the Crimean War and, soon after that, of the Indian Mutiny, both of which occurred during his headship. Soon he would have learned of the deaths of some Old Twyfordians, including those of Colonel Lowth and Captain Connelly in the Crimea, and of Captain Garrett and Henry Faithfull during the Indian Mutiny.

At about the same time there is mention in the scrapbook of another Old Boy – Sir Richmond Shakespeare of the Indian Cavalry – 'who rescued the prisoners after the Kabul disaster'. Central Asia has, for a long time, proved a difficult part of the world for the British to influence.

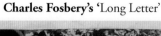

Charles Fosbery's 'Long Letter'

J.H Dodgson . Richardson . Gordon . E.Dodgson . Fosbery . J.Fredrick . A. Heathcote .

This photograph, taken by Charles Dodgson, shows Charles Fosbery (*third from the right*) as well as Dodgson's cousin, Jimmy (*left*), and his youngest brother, Edwin (*centre*).

In the Millennium Year, 2000, the Bursar received a small package from Canada which contained a cylindrical pot. It had been sent by a descendant of Charles Fosbery who was a boy at Twyford with G.W. Kitchin in the late 1850s.

The pot contained a rolled-up letter over 13 feet long and barely one and a half inches wide for the whole of that length. It is made up of 23 individual strips of paper each securely pasted to the previous one. It was obviously written after the pasting-together had been completed and, although the first few words are missing, it is thought that it had been sent to his brother, Henry, who was still at home.

Some extracts from the Long Letter *are shown on the opposite page, printed actual size.*

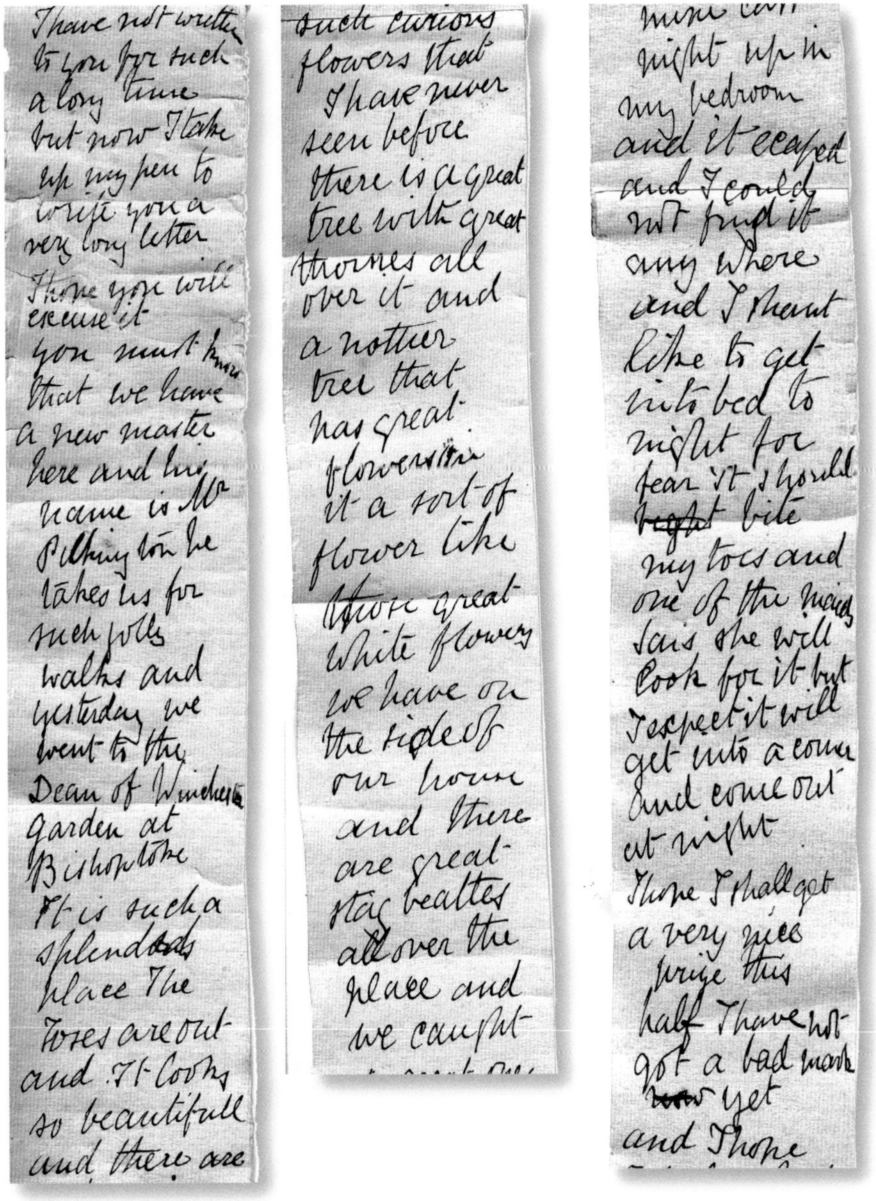

Column 1 (handwritten):
I have not written to you for such a long time but now I take up my pen to write you a very long letter I hope you will excuse it you must know that we have a new master here and his name is Mr Pilkington he takes us for such jolly walks and yesterday we went to the Dean of Winchester garden at Bishopstoke It is such a splendid place The roses are out and it looks so beautifull and there are

Column 2 (handwritten):
such curious flowers that I have never seen before there is a great tree with great thornes all over it and a nother tree that has great flowers on it a sort of flower like those great white flowers we have on the side of our house and there are great stag beatles all over the place and we caught

Column 3 (handwritten):
mine last night up in my bedroom and it escaped and I could not find it any where and I meant like to get into bed to night for fear it should bite my toes and one of the maids says she will look for it but I expect it will get into a corner and come out at night I hope I shall get a very nice prize this half I have not got a bad mark yet and I hope

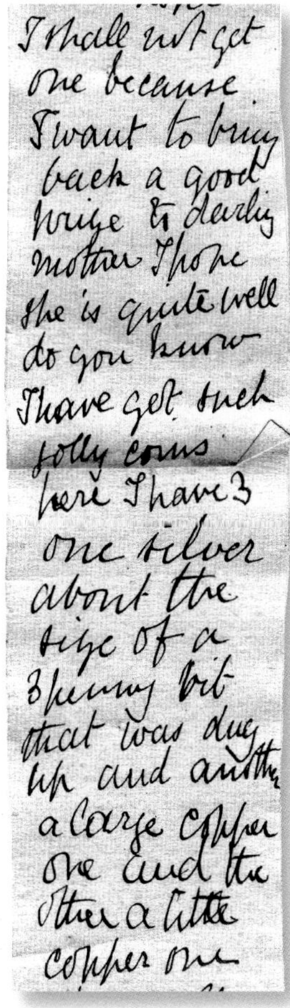

Column 4 (handwritten):
I shall not get one because I want to bring back a good prize to dearly mother I hope she is quite well do you know I have got such jolly coins here I have 3 one silver about the size of a 3 penny bit that was dug up and another a large copper one and the other a little copper one

Short extracts from Fosbery's 'Long Letter' opposite:

'I have not written to you for such a long time but now I take up my pen to write to you a very long letter. I hope you will excuse it.
You must know that we have a new master here and his name is Mr Pilkington. He takes us for such jolly walks and yesterday we went to the Dean of Winchester's garden at Bishopstoke. It is such a splendid place. The roses are out and it looks so beautiful and there are such curious flowers that I have never seen before...
'...and there are great stag beetles all over the place and we caught 4 great ones, and I took mine last night up in my bedroom and it escaped and I could not find it anywhere and I shan't like to get into bed tonight for fear it should bite my toes, and one of the maids says she will look for it, but I expect it will get into a corner and come out at night...'

The Revd Latham Wickham, son of the Revd Robert Wickham, became Headmaster in January 1862. We have less detailed information about his 26 years as Headmaster than we have of the Revd Kitchin's seven years, because Mr Wickham's records, if ever they existed, have not survived.

With games becoming part of regular school life, extra land was purchased and more of the field in front of the main house was cleared and improved. Nevertheless, it was amongst the buildings that the majority of changes were to be made between 1862 and 1887.

As Latham Wickham's family increased (he had six children) and the number of pupils grew, he felt it would be sensible to make more provision for possible sickness. Accordingly, in about 1865 he built the ground floor Matron's Room with rooms over it, providing some accommodation for single masters.

Next came what Latham Wickham would have considered to have been his greatest contribution to Twyford – the building of the School Chapel, dedicated in June 1869.

Prior to that the boys had attended the Sunday morning service in Twyford Parish Church, sitting in a damp and chilly side chapel and, from Mr Kitchin's day onwards, a Sunday service held by the Headmaster in the Old Schoolroom (now known as Upper School). Mr Wickham had also taken to holding Sunday evening prayers in the Dining Hall over the roadside kitchen and it is likely that short daily prayers were held there too.

The new purpose-built Chapel was later to be extended at its western end and embellished in several respects, but the main part of this lovely little place of worship – an unusual asset for a prep school of that day – was the vision and creation of Latham Wickham.

Mr Wickham was to make two other significant additions to the School. To start with, Twyford's first gymnasium was erected between the main house and Upper School. Then, in 1878, after 19 years of marriage, Mrs Wickham sadly died. However, within two years Mr Wickham had remarried and, remarkably, was building a large two-storey extension to the west of the main house.

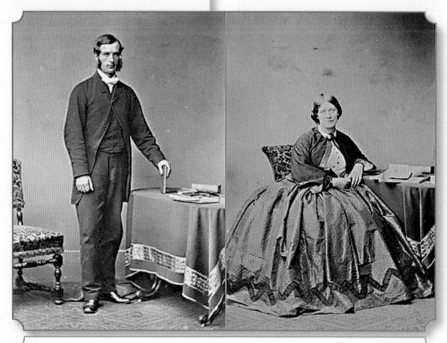

The Revd and Mrs Latham Wickham
These pictures show Latham Wickham and his first wife, Harriette, photographed shortly after their marriage in 1859. They were to have six children before she died from TB at the age of 41.

The first Gymnasium – built c1877
This picture shows Latham Wickham's gymnasium, drawn by his son, Charles. The new gymnasium had four pointed gables and was built on the site of the Cloister and Inner Court that used to separate Upper School from the main school building.

The Chapel – before 1895
This early picture of the Chapel shows it as originally built. The organ is adjacent to the altar and the super-reredos and altar rails have yet to be installed. The pews, lectern, tiling and hanging lamps that we know today are all in place.

The School House
The main house as it was in 1857 (*top*) and, later, in the 1880s, shortly after the extension was built. Latham Wickham's addition, which provided him with a large study with an extra bedroom above it, is set back on the left of the house. The study has been used as the School Office since the 1980s. A glazed conservatory ran along the southern side. The tiled floor can still be seen today, together with the timber plate to which the sloping roof of the conservatory was fixed.

Photographs of Latham Wickham show a rather serious young man and, later, a severe-looking bearded gentleman, typical of the popular image of an upright and rather humourless Victorian headmaster. Nevertheless, many of his pupils had kind memories of him, and Kitchin's commendation to parents, that the Revd Latham Wickham 'is an energetic and upright man, and most anxious for the welfare of the boys' seems to have been borne out as accurate throughout his long tenure.

Mr Kitchin had organised days out to reward good behaviour. These usually took the form of picnics at Shawford Park or in the New Forest, or even an excursion in a steamer round the Isle of Wight; at least once there had been a visit to Bournemouth, which was still a country resort. Latham Wickham continued this tradition of what were known as 'reward days'. For instance, he hired a steamer which took the boys, who had earned this privilege, to Seaview on the Isle of Wight where they landed for a swim from the beach 'while servants prepared dinner in the shade'. Such outings were organised regularly, providing thoughtful boys with a strong incentive to avoid the dreaded assessments *male* and *pessime*.

Summers might well have been having a trial run for global warming in Kitchin's

Seaview 'Ahoy'!

and Latham Wickham's day because it became so hot having school meals in the Dining Hall over the kitchen that they both took to having tables and chairs erected in the nearby garden for midday meals, shaded by a tarpaulin. When this wore out Latham had a wooden-framed tent made to take its place.

There have been periodical renewals of canvas and, occasionally, of sections of the frame (especially after the tempestuous storm on the night of 15/16 October 1987 when 15 million trees were blown down across the south of England) but, for at least the next 130 years, the marquee, or tent, proved to be remarkably useful.

School Photograph c1887
Latham Wickham retired soon after this picture was taken. He is the rather formidable man with a white beard and mortar board in the rear row. Sitting in front of him is most probably his daughter, Susan Harriette, and to her left, his second wife, Charlotte.

.... for hot summer days

Latham Wickham's detailed written records may not exist but, to compensate for that, modern Twyfordians daily live with his legacy whether they visit the Matron's Room or School Office, sing hymns in the Chapel, sleep in North Room or look after guests at a match tea in the marquee.

Sadly, Latham's health was not robust and at the end of 1887 he turned over the ownership and headship of the School to his son, Charles Townshend Wickham – usually referred to as C.T.W. – another alumnus of Christ Church, Oxford.

Latham, aged 54, then retired to become vicar of a small parish in North Wales near the home of his first wife's family.

His attitude to education had been sound and traditional rather than innovative so, in a way, the School might have been ready for a change of leadership.

Pavilion Scenes

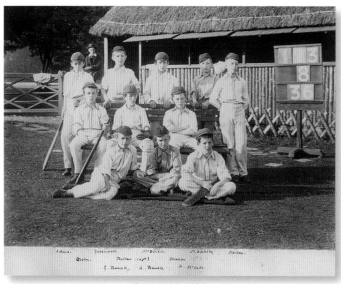

Cricket XI 1894

The team is posing in front of the thatched pavilion which is also the backdrop for the picture (*below*) of the ponies. The boy in the centre of the rear row of the cricket team is H.C. McDonell, who was to become Headmaster of the School in 1910 and who played 78 times for Hampshire between 1908 and 1921.

Jenny, Fred, and Hebe c1893
Hebe (*right*), an old bay mare, came to Twyford for her later years in 1886 and was put to work mowing, pumping well water and pulling a dogcart. Fred, the garden boy, looked after the ponies and Jenny was Hebe's companion.

The Revd Charles Wickham – only 26 years of age and newly ordained – needed all the strength and quiet confidence that many Twyfordians will have seen in the fine portrait of him by a parent – Philip de Laszlo – displayed in the School for many years.

The two main problems faced by C.T.W. – a shortage of pupils and a diphtheria epidemic – were, luckily, separated by some eight years: together they might have proved too much to overcome.

The first difficulty was a classic one for a small school – falling numbers. C.T.W. took over a roll of 43 boys, which within two years had dropped to 37. At one stage during this period, 27 of these boys went down with measles: fortunately on this occasion all recovered. Prior to C.T.W.'s arrival, Twyford had been one of a very small number of true preparatory schools. Now things were changing and there was increasing competition. It probably had not helped that Latham Wickham, for most of his headship, had refused to let boys compete for scholarships. He feared the dangers of cramming and overwork. In the new climate of competition encouraged by the foundation of new schools, this attitude had to, and did, change.

Such change takes time to bear fruit and in the meantime economies were called for. For example, today we can see a small square of floorboarding in the north east corner of the Old Dining Hall that is of a different colour from the main part of the timber floor. This is where Charles Wickham installed a lift to raise food to the Dining Hall from the kitchen below. This lift cost £8: the 'Butler and Boy' that it replaced had cost Mr Wickham £52 per annum in wages. One hopes that the butler and his assistant soon found other employment nearby. Meanwhile a retiring assistant master was not replaced. Numbers then stabilised and gradually began to increase.

The Revd Charles Wickham

Headmaster 1888-1910

The younger man…

…and the older man.

A portrait painted by Philip de Laszlo, a Twyford parent, and noted society portrait painter during the early 20th century

With economies made and finances improving, Charles Wickham took into partnership his Second Master, Mr H.C. Strahan (a former headmaster of St George's School, Ascot, for whom C.T.W. had worked not long before). Mr Strahan was to be 'Headmaster in Partnership' with Mr Wickham from 1890 to 1896.

The house, Mallard's Close, tucked into the corner of the main bend of Bourne Lane, had recently been built for the use of Mr Strahan and his family. However, he decided to live at The Cottage, adjacent to the main School entrance, because it was nearer to the School buildings. Mallard's Close was then let.

The Cottage c1857

The Cottage, at the entrance to the School, has changed very little in appearance over the past 150 years. It has been used mainly for staff accommodation, although it was designated as the Sick House for a period after the infections of 1896 and 1897.

Headmasters in Partnership 1890

Both Heads (*centre of back row*) cut quite a dash in their different ways, with Mr Strahan's tweed jacket and cap making a particularly individual statement for those days.

Like his predecessor, G.W. Kitchin, Charles Wickham had been keeping a scrapbook, which is in the School archives. However, in 1895 he and Mr Strahan allowed two masters, Mr M.R. Bethune and the Revd G.G.T. Heywood, to put together a termly record of events in the School: this was the beginning of *The Twyfordian.*

Consequently we enjoy a nearly unbroken record of life in the School and the activities of our forebears, from the time that C.T.W. made his first scrapbook entry in January 1888.

THE TWYFORDIAN.

| Vol. I. | JANUARY, 1895. | No. 1. |

INTRODUCTORY.

We have often been asked whether we have a School paper, and if not, why not? We have generally rather brusquely put the question aside. Nothing worth recording! Merely a means of advertisement! Don't want small boys to think when they make a score at cricket of its appearance in print! and various other such reasons as might occur to our minds at the time. But for all our apparent assurance we have at times felt a qualm lest our want of a paper was backed by very inadequate reasons indeed. We have recollections of a School paper with which we were connected, a short account of which may

In the early 1890s, changes were made inside the School that were probably intended to provide a healthier and more modern environment. For example, improvements were made to the dormitories, and from then onwards morning and evening washing – previously done in the old washing room on the ground floor – were to take place upstairs. Daily life was made more comfortable by a change of dress: Eton suits – for some time regulation wear for most boys throughout the week – now had to be worn only on Sundays. This remained the situation until 1914 after which Eton suits never returned.

South of Mallard's Close lay an agricultural field – later, in 2007, to be the site of the new all weather pitch. With an increasing interest in games and the first inter-prep school cricket matches being arranged, C.T.W. decided to grass this area. This would be known as the Barley Field for nearly 100 years.

A library and museum were established, and collections of butterflies, stamps and fossils were positively encouraged. A single master's flat was built above the lobby just inside the boys' front entrance, to the west of Upper School. The first occupant was to be Mr Heywood who, as we have already remarked, was starting up *The Twyfordian* with a colleague. Mr Heywood was generally recognised to be Charles Wickham's successor-designate as Headmaster.

However, Charles' main project at that time was the enlargement and improvement of the Chapel, built by his father some 25 years earlier. With financial help from 214 kind subscribers, the fine carved oak super-reredos behind the altar was fitted and the three small dormer windows on the south side (incorporating some old stained glass) were constructed to improve the light. Additionally, an organ chamber was added on to the north side to house the organ, and the whole western end was extended, providing the

The beautiful carved oak super-reredos placed above the Chapel altar in 1895 was the work of George Herbert Kitchin, architect and artist, (1866-1951), son of the former Headmaster G.W. Kitchin. As a designer, Herbert Kitchin contributed enormously to the School in subsequent years.

vestry and the seating that is immediately inside the door. This was a great and successful project, celebrated by a service of dedication to mark the re-opening of the Chapel on 25 June 1895.

An immediate effect on the life of the School was the formation of the School Choir – taking advantage of the enlargement of the Chapel and the existence of a better organ. It is a happy thought that 114 years later the choir would sing in Winchester Cathedral to celebrate the bicentenary of the move from Segar's Buildings to the 'small but elegant Queen Anne house situated near the vicarage'.

Choir Expedition, July 1895
With the enlargement of the Chapel a choir of leading voices was formed. In order to compensate them for the extra time given to choir practice – ½ an hour per day instead of ¾ hour per week – a day's holiday was given to the members and an expedition made to the New Forest. (*photographer G.G.T. Heywood*)

The Longley Cup

The Longley Cup was instituted in 1894, when it was presented by Colonel A.W. Longley, an Old Twyfordian of 1851. It was awarded annually to the best all-round athlete, for his performance in football, cricket, gymnastics and athletics, but in recent years has been awarded to the winning house. However, from 2010, the Cup will be awarded on Sports Day to the boy or girl who scores most points for their house. G.P. Burrell, the first winner (*shown here*), was a member of an Alton brewing family. In the First World War he served in the Hampshire Regiment and won the MC in Mesopotamia. Major Burrell wrote articles for *The Field* and one year bred the champion terrier of all England. He also invented a humane killer for rats and vermin. He died in 1931 at Alton.

'Theatricals', December 1894
The cast of *Bombastes Furioso*, a satirical drama with comic songs, which was popular throughout the 19th century.

As the boys departed for their Christmas holiday in December 1895, Charles Wickham could understandably look back on the previous eight years of his headship with some satisfaction.

End of term about 1900
The carriages are probably taking the boys to Shawford railway station.

The style of education was beginning to change. Hitherto, it had been heavily classical. As we have seen, Greek and Latin were central elements in the curriculum. They were taught in what we now would consider to be a most unimaginative way. C.T.W. had, however, introduced 'modern' subjects, to prepare boys for the 'modern' side of public schools and for entering the Royal Navy. Whilst the classics were still dominant, there was a move towards the acceptance of maths, science and modern languages as being of equal importance.

After Latham Wickham's discouragement of the hard work involved in preparing for scholarships and bursaries, some boys were beginning to be successful in gaining such awards.

The teaching staff was of a high calibre – and the domestic and grounds staff stable and loyal: the three gardeners C. Ingram, G. Smith and T. Spratt had already worked at the School for 25, 30 and 31 years respectively. The School pony was no longer confined to pumping water for the School's brew-house as in Bedford's day; now, most of the mowing of the playing fields was done by a gang mower drawn by the pony which wore leather shoes to protect the grass.

The public schools, fed by preparatory schools such as Twyford, were educating boys fit for the professions, the Army or Navy, the Church, or for the administration of Britain's huge global enterprise – the British Empire. Queen Victoria's Diamond Jubilee Fleet Review in 1897 at Spithead, attended by the boys, displayed the might of the Royal Navy – including 22 battleships based in home waters. Fifty years later, the sun was setting on the Empire, and the day of the battleship was almost over.

A visit to the battleship HMS Duke of York in 1947

At Twyford, C.T.W.'s greatest problem lay ahead: the worst two years of the School's history were about to commence.

At times during 1896 and 1897, Charles Wickham may have reflected on an episode some years earlier, when one of the master's wives had been gravely ill, as had one of the boys. The cause was suspected to have been a blocked drain beneath the School washroom. Sanitary engineers had been called in and had remedied the immediate problem, but their recommendations for renewal of the sanitary system were so extensive that the full scheme had not been carried out.

In January 1896, now back at School from their holidays, several boys contracted sore throats. In a few days the number had increased to 27. Some of these boys became very ill and little Dick Burrell died on 19 February, followed four days later, by his closest friend, Malcolm Johnston. Brass memorial plaques in the Chapel commemorate them. They were both ten years old.

Those boys who were still fit were evacuated to the nearby homes of kind local friends, with many being accommodated at the Bridge Inn, Shawford. They were taught in a big room over the inn's stables. Some of the fit boys were then taken ill and returned to the School: the dreaded word 'diphtheria' was now pronounced. As and when boys became well enough to travel, they were sent home. Those convalescents who could not go home for one reason or another were sent, with two masters, to a cottage on Hayling Island, lent by a parent.

As the School buildings could not be used until certified as safe by the public health authorities, a lease was obtained for two months from Lord Northbrook (an Old Twyfordian and former Viceroy of India) of Westfields in Winchester, later to be the preparatory school West Downs. Westfields had previously been a school and so was

ideal, but it was never popular with the Twyfordians who felt it to be too large and impersonal.

By the end of May 1896, the immediate remedial works required having been completed, the Medical Officer had given the 'all clear' and the whole School returned to Twyford. Sadly, however, parents' confidence in the School had been shaken and the roll of 56 boys, pre-diphtheria, had now dwindled to 30.

Westfields, Romsey Road, Winchester
– to which Twyford was evacuated for a few weeks in 1896 (*above*).
It later became the prep school, West Downs, which closed in 1988.

The building, pictured below in 2008, has since been renovated and has become part of the new University of Winchester.

Despite the return to Twyford from Westfields on 28 May 1896 with sorely depleted numbers, the newly founded magazine, *The Twyfordian,* reports a fairly normal Summer term.

The tent – or marquee – was put up on 15 June for meals to be taken in a cooler atmosphere than that provided in the Dining Hall over the main School kitchen: the death is recorded of Mr Thomas Hughes, Q.C., the author of *Tom Brown's Schooldays,* who had been at Twyford from 1830 to 1833, before he went to Rugby: plans had been prepared for a new (and large) sanatorium which would be built straightaway 'in the south west corner of the cricket field'. This would avoid the need for the main School house to become, itself, a form of isolation hospital as had recently been the case. Originally intended to be called Tripp's Hill from the old name of the site, it actually took the name of the adjacent section of the main road, Serle's Hill.

Autumn Term 1896 started normally but in mid-November the dreaded symptom of sore throats recurred and at the end of the month all the healthy boys were sent home followed, in mid-December, by the infected boys.

The public health authorities firmly recommended that no boys should return to the School until a major reconstruction of the old buildings had been completed. Charles Wickham then moved very fast indeed, and within a few days had leased a vacant country house in Sussex for a whole year. By 26 January 1897 staff and boys had assembled in Emsworth House, Copthorne, between East Grinstead and the hamlet of Gatwick – a remarkable feat of organisation.

The Copthorne exile seems to have been a happy period. The School was welcomed by the local people – be they the gardeners at the house or local grandees, station-master or proprietor of the Station Hotel (with his handy horse-drawn dogcarts), local sports

Emsworth House, Copthorne 1897

clubs or Sussex preparatory schools. And it was at Copthorne that, in company with the local inhabitants, the boys could enjoy the lighting of a great bonfire to celebrate Queen Victoria's Jubilee Day. Forty other bonfires were visible from Copthorne, and a hearty rendering of *God Save the Queen* boosted by the efforts of the new School Choir helped to mark the Queen's six decades on the throne.

Whilst School life was continuing as normally as possible at Copthorne, Mr Wickham must have been a familiar sight as he travelled between East Grinstead and Shawford railway stations. While running the School in exile, he was overseeing an extensive building reconstruction programme back at Twyford. Not only was the new sanatorium, Serle's Hill, being built but, of greater immediate importance, the inner part of the main School house was being gutted, opened up and modernised.

The most visible feature of this work, as seen today, is Central Hall. This area had been dark, cramped and ill-ventilated. It had contained, amongst various nooks and crannies in which small boys could hide, the boot-room (doubtless rather smelly) and a modest boys' washing room – for daytime use – which would seldom have dried out properly.

Now these unattractive spaces were cleared away. A fine, wide staircase was built, leading from a spacious ground floor hall to a first floor landing area, well lit by new skylights and high windows above.

Better arrangements were made for boots and washing, and all manner of other functional and practical changes (both of uses and names) were made within the old building. In particular, some dormitory ceilings were raised and windows enlarged to relieve the previous dark and airless atmosphere. The resultant loss of headroom meant that the old attic bedrooms became lumber rooms and water tank space – and gone (if it had ever really existed!) was the legendary 'prison'.

The most important point of attack was, however, an entirely new system of drainage. Work had been carried out in 1896 but now, in 1897, the School's drains having been condemned, were being totally replaced. However, Charles Wickham's successor as Headmaster, Harold McDonell, would still prefer the earth closet system to that of the water closet!

Nevertheless, thanks largely to the financial generosity of Charles Wickham's father, Latham, the School was modernised and well prepared for the new century.

It was probably a myth, but it was said that the Revd Liscombe Clarke, who had the School for a short while before Mr Bedford came in 1815, used part of the attics over the rear of the main house as a 'prison' for naughty boys.

In *Vanity Fair*, written at the same time, Thackeray tells of a 'black hole' at Miss Pinkerton's Academy at Chiswick. Perhaps such arrangements were part of the disciplinary system of the day!

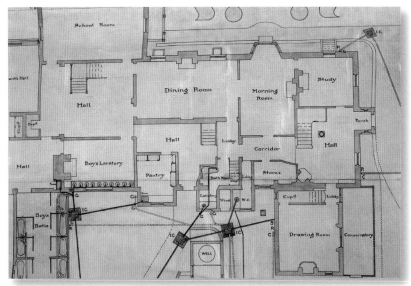

House Layout 1912
A large scroll, drawn in fine detail and entitled *Plan shewing Drains Laid 1897 and 1912*, shows the drains and a plan of the buildings. The extract illustrates the layout of the interior of the front of the School at that time.

It must have been a marvellous moment for the Revd and Mrs Charles Wickham when they received the returning boys at the old, but refurbished, School on Thursday, 20 January 1898: as they did so, the Parish Church bells rang a welcoming, and much appreciated, peal.

In a spirit of confidence it was decided that Serle's Hill – the big new building, designed to be a sanatorium and just completed – would be too big for that purpose and would be let as a private residence. Meanwhile, sick boys would be cared for nearer to the main School in The Cottage, which was now nominated as the Sick House, having been vacated by Mr Strahan in 1896.

School life quickly settled back into its former routine, although Mr Wickham decided not to organise sports matches against other schools for the first term back. All that the Headmaster and staff wanted was a quiet – and healthy – life for a while. Nevertheless, games and outdoor activities were not totally neglected. Two new thatched sports pavilions were built; there was fierce competition for the Longley Cup; golf enjoyed one of its periodic crazes, and was played around the School grounds by both staff and boys; and walks towards Hazeley Down became more interesting because of the building of the new waterworks beside the road.

Swimming was encouraged and a section of the River Itchen was dredged and graded: boards were fitted beside the bank and canvas screens were erected as wind breaks and to provide some privacy. Even low diving boards were constructed.

In the outside world, 29 Old Twyfordians who had joined the Army found themselves embroiled in the South African War fought against the Boers. Two weeks before the turn of the century, such an Old Twyfordian, Captain Walter Congreve, won the Victoria Cross – the country's highest award for gallantry in the face of the enemy. Congreve remained a successful and resolute soldier as will

The Bathing Place

Swimming on the River Itchen about 1900. The river was used for swimming from the 1850s until the new Swimming Bath was built in 1914.

'A capital Bathing Place has been made in the river below the Church, and constant use has been made of it during the last month of Term.'
The Twyfordian, July 1900

be clear from a report in *The Twyfordian* some 17 years later when, in 1917, as Lieut Gen Sir Walter Congreve, VC, KCB, MVO, he was wounded in action.

Finally, the very end of the nineteenth century saw the cutting of a link with its earliest years, when the death was announced, in his 90th year, of the oldest known former Twyfordian. This was of the Revd W. Bigg-Wither who used to recall that the news of the great victory at Waterloo, in 1815, was received whilst he was a boy at the School.

Roberts and Congreve heading for the guns!

The Victoria Cross awarded to Captain Congreve.

Captain W. N. Congreve VC

Captain Walter Congreve, of the Rifle Brigade, who had entered Twyford in 1874, received the Victoria Cross for an act of conspicuous courage at the Battle of Colenso in South Africa on 15 December 1899.

The Boers were about to take possession of a number of British artillery guns, having mowed down the gunners and horses. Captains Congreve and Schofield, and Lieutenant Frederick Roberts, son of the Commander-in-Chief, South Africa (later Field Marshal Earl Roberts), seeing this, rode into what was spoken of as a perfect hail of bullets, and, with the help of some remarkably courageous and cool-headed NCOs and drivers, brought back two of the guns.

Sadly, Roberts, having been rescued by Congreve when hit, later died of his wounds.

Five Victoria Crosses and 19 Distinguished Conduct Medals were awarded to British soldiers for this outstanding action.

Congreve later became a General in the Great War (1914-1918): quite remarkably his son also won a Victoria Cross – but he had not been to Twyford. Gallantry, though, was certainly in the Congreve genes.

Having concluded the story of the nineteenth century with a report of the death of a former Twyfordian, it is unfortunate that the entry of the School into the new century was soon to be similarly marked. The national mood was sombre following the death of the elderly Queen Victoria in early 1901, after 63 years on the throne; the whole School had seats in Winchester Cathedral for the Memorial Service. Then, in September of that year, the Revd Latham Wickham, father of the Headmaster, died at the age of 68. He had been Headmaster himself for 26 years and the important contributions that he had made to the School have already been described.

Both the Queen and Latham Wickham had enjoyed reasonable spans of life, but it was a terrible shock for the School when the young master, Mr Heywood, died unexpectedly at his home at the School, Mallard's Close, in June 1902, after a few days' seemingly innocuous illness. He was only 32 years of age and had come to Twyford soon after taking his degree at Trinity College, Cambridge. He had been ordained priest by the Bishop of Winchester in 1899, and had, subsequently, given to the School the brass and oak altar rail in the Chapel to mark both his

ordination and his appointment as Chaplain to Twyford School.

Mr Heywood had been devoted to the School and had applied all his energies to its success, in particular being of great support during the difficult Copthorne evacuation year.

Fra Angelico Angels

With the loss of Latham Wickham and Mr Heywood within nine months – both of whom had had deep emotional and practical connections with the Chapel – thoughts turned quickly as to how their contributions could be properly commemorated. As a result, subscription lists were opened for 'The Heywood Memorial' which was to take the form of major improvements to the east end of the Chapel, and for 'The Latham Wickham Memorial Window' – to be at the western end.

The Revd Heywood's memorial consists of the ten painted angels that line the sanctuary. They are copies of Fra Angelico's famous set of angels, beautifully executed by Signora M. Franceschi, a well-known Florentine copyist. Heywood had felt strongly that richness and colour were important accessories of worship: the choice of memorial therefore seemed very appropriate.

The memorial for Latham Wickham was to be the replacement of the west window that he had had carved when he built the Chapel in 1869. Because of a mistake by the stonemason at the time, he had never been entirely happy with it. When Charles Wickham had extended the Chapel to the west in 1895, that original west window had been re-erected in the extension. Now, as Latham's memorial, that slightly unsatisfactory situation was to be put right.

The work was put into the hands of Mr C.E. Kempe, himself an Old Twyfordian, and, after Burne-Jones, possibly the most notable of the pre-Raphaelite school of glass painters. The four-light window depicts St Christopher carrying the Child Christ; St Nicholas, the patron saint of children; St John the Baptist, the patron saint of the Chapel; and William of Wykeham, a patron of education and reputed ancestor of the Wickham family.

An interesting fact of detail is that all Kempe's designs incorporate a small painted wheatsheaf: this can be seen on the left edge of the window near St Christopher's right foot. Even today the journal of The Kempe Society is called 'The Wheatsheaf'.

With the memorials completed, two services of dedication were held in 1903: that for 'The Heywood Memorial' on 23 June, and the service for 'The Latham Wickham Memorial Window' on 29 October. Certainly, both men would have been gratified by these memorials.

The West Window of the Chapel

The Revd Heywood

The boys had clearly liked Mr Heywood and felt his loss, as shown in this rather touching letter home (*shown right*), written by (George) Marsden Roberts. In typical schoolboy fashion Master Roberts asks his father to persuade Mr Wickham ('Charlie'!) to grant a half-holiday in honour of the Coronation!

Marsden Roberts was a son of Dr George Roberts, the local physician, who, it is said, owned the first motor vehicle in Twyford. Young Marsden, boarding at the School, used to feel very cross seeing his father driving up and down Bourne Lane. As a result when his turn came, he did not send his son, Michael, to Twyford School to avoid such a situation arising again. Michael, in due course, also became a respected doctor in Twyford and in his later years painted the picture of Segar's depicted earlier in this book.

With the coming of the new century Charles Wickham took his place as one of the influential figures in the independent educational world, and served as Chairman of the Association of Preparatory Schools in 1904. Public schools were multiplying in number as were the preparatory schools needed to prepare the children for them. As we know, Twyford School was in existence long before prep schools, as such, began to be founded, but, by C.T.W.'s day, there were many establishments – of which Twyford was but one – offering parents the best chance of getting their offspring into the public school of their choice.

Early in the new century the establishment of a Common Entrance Examination for most public schools was under discussion and there were a great many verbal battles between the 'conservatives' and the 'progressives' over the importance, in such an examination, of compulsory Latin and Greek.

Charles Wickham was one of the 'progressives' – a true forerunner of his nephew, Bob Wickham, who was to be such an influential supporter of the teaching of science and technology in prep schools half a century later. Because of Twyford's long-term connection with the older public schools, the School would have been well-known and the opinions of its headmaster respected. In a slightly different field, C.T.W.'s experience with the great epidemic and the remedial works that followed, would have been useful to fellow headmasters if they had similar problems – not unlikely at the time.

Triple Lantern
This triple lens magic lantern, which belonged to Mr Marsh, dates from about 1880, and is one of three magic lanterns that remain on display in the School. There is also a collection of slides, comprising worthy cultural sights, and children's slides with ingenious mechanisms to produce apparent movement in the projected image.

Nevertheless, despite being influential in the broader educational world, Charles Wickham and the School had to be successful in their own right. Probably the most important factor in ensuring such success was the appointment around this period of some absolutely first-class staff, several of whom served the School for practically all their teaching careers, without, it seems, becoming old fashioned or stale.

Another thing – seemingly small, but in practice having a great influence on the boys' attitudes to more formal learning – was the marvellous variety of extra-curricular talks and activities. For example, between 1900 and 1916, the Revd Theodore Wood, who was a highly talented and entertaining lecturer, gave a regular series of original and exciting talks illustrated by brilliantly coloured drawings on blackboards. An example of one of his facts was: 'a human house built on the same scale as an ant's nest would have to be 3½ miles high and 2½ miles across'; and one of his questions to his audience was: 'how many feet of worm does a cock robin catch in a morning's hunting?'

Add to visitors such as this, the home-grown wonders of Mr George Marsh, an Old Twyfordian and master at the School, who was to devote most of his life to Twyford. He had a boy-level interest in all aspects of the burgeoning scientific world of those days and, in common with Dr Roberts, owned a motorised tricycle that much intrigued the boys. He also entertained them with lectures on all sorts of subjects which would have provided interesting titbits for their letters home.

Dr George Roberts aboard his motorised tricycle in 1897. His son, Marsden, a boarder at the School, did not like seeing his father drive along Bourne Lane as it made him homesick.

By 1904 the number of boys in the School had risen steadily to just over 50. This return to comparative prosperity enabled Charles Wickham to make further additions and several improvements to the School buildings.

Upper School – originally the main Schoolroom – had deteriorated over the years. The reason was this: as we have seen, in 1877, part of the space between the main house and Upper School, which formerly had been an open Inner Court alongside a covered cloister (or passage), was roofed over to accommodate the first gymnasium. Sixteen years later, in 1893, C.T.W. had decided that he needed to develop that space by pulling down the gymnasium and replacing it with classrooms and, over them, a dormitory – New School Room – and a single master's flat.

Because C.T.W. now had more flexible classroom arrangements, Upper School was no longer needed for teaching and the gymnasium equipment, such as it was, was transferred into it. Woodwork was also taught in Upper School and there is a photograph in *The Twyfordian* of March 1901, entitled 'The Carpenters Shop' showing a woodwork class in action, with gym equipment overhanging the work benches: it is, in fact, Upper School.

Charles Wickham always felt guilty about this misuse of the original big Schoolroom and took steps to correct matters. Accordingly, he erected a large 'temporary' corrugated iron building, lined with timber, to become the gymnasium. It was aligned east-west across what is now the southern part of the western courtyard. It was eventually demolished with the building of the new Sports Hall in 1989. C.T.W. must also have found somewhere else for the woodwork classes to take place, for he soon persuaded over 140 well-wishers to subscribe towards a very successful renovation of Upper School in 1906. The oak panelling on the walls was restored,

and the room was furnished with oak tables and benches which are still in use around the School to this day.

Upper School
(*above*) The Carpenters' Shop and Gym 1901; and (*below*) after the 1906 restoration.

Charles Wickham's other main additions were the classroom on the left as one moves up the two well-worn steps approaching Upper School, and a new fives court, eventually demolished (after a spell as a girls' changing room) in 1999 to make room for the southern part of the new Science School.

Finally, a minor but interesting item from *The Twyfordian* of December 1902: 'The Dormitories have had their names put up over the doors. Anyone not knowing the name of his Dormitory for the future will be considered "a vagrant"; it is not known what will happen to him.' (These are the painted name boards that are still in place today.)

Upper School Steps
Upper School had been built by Mr Bedford in 1819. It is very likely that these steps led up to its original entrance porch. If so, these steps have been worn away by Twyfordian soles for over 190 years.

Charles Wickham's 'temporary' gymnasium (*left*), photographed from the first phase of the new classrooms in 1991, looking towards the back of the old School – and in 2010 (*right*). Note the new dwarf walls with their lights showing in both pictures.

Throughout the decade after the School's return from its year in the wilderness at Copthorne in Sussex, things went well. Concerts were ambitious, a fair proportion of matches were won, boys passed into the better public schools – sometimes with awards – and the buildings were steadily improved. Old Twyfordians sent back fascinating, if hair-raising, accounts of their lives serving King and Country a long way from home – for example, in China fighting the Boxer rebels, and on the North West Frontier of India in actions against encroaching Afghan tribesmen.

Less dramatic but still highly important struggles were, meanwhile, taking place back in Britain itself. Here is a short extract from *The Twyfordian* of December 1908:

> ## TO THE EDITOR.
>
> DEAR SIR,—We hope you will like a short account of the Bonfire and Fireworks this year. The Guy was a Suffragette; she wore a brown Norfolk jacket, a brown skirt, a many-coloured tie, a pair of old football boots, and had a pair of eyeglasses on. She held a banner on which was printed in large letters "Votes for Women." At five minutes past five the seniors carried the Guy down to the bonfire, and the rest of the school followed soon after. The gardeners then carried her up to the top of the Bonfire, and tied her there. Then they thoroughly drenched her with paraffin. When all was ready the four youngest boys in the school, Turner, Tom Sergeant, Leslie, and Goodger, lit the Bonfire. It caught very easily and reached the Guy much sooner than usual. Very soon afterwards she, and the pole to which she was tied, fell amidst cheers. At about 5.30

It is not necessary to continue the description but this is included because, to have any value, even a brief historical account such as this should describe life of the time, 'warts and all'. The contrast of the Bonfire Night report with a long article in the next issue of

The Suffragette Guy 1908
'Martyr'd for the cause amidst popular derision' was the caption against this photograph in the album.

The Twyfordian about the wonderful work done by Dr Barnardo's Homes is, to modern eyes, a strange one. However these were the attitudes prevailing as the School approached the centenary of its move to the current site.

To mark this important occasion, Charles Wickham, firstly, hoped to arrange for the publication of a history of the School: accordingly, he wrote to parents asking, in advance, for subscribers who would help with the likely costs. This help was forthcoming and *The Story of Twyford School* was duly compiled and published.

Secondly, C.T.W. planned a day of celebration to be held at the School on 24 June 1909. This was to be his final big event as Headmaster and appears to have been a most successful and enjoyable one.

The Centenary Celebrations held on 24 June 1909

Leaflets describing *The Story of Twyford School* had been sent to those 700 Old Twyfordians whose addresses were known, as a result of which some 400 requests for copies had been received. All these applicants were then invited to a day of celebrations at the School.

The morning started with Services in the Chapel for the School and household only, followed closely by the start of the traditional annual cricket match – Twyford School v 'Patres'. In due course rain forced a draw but, even so, over 300 runs were scored in the day.

As the fathers tried to outwit their sons on the cricket field, other guests began to gather. The motor car was not yet dominant as the means of personal transport and *The Twyfordian* tells how probably the majority of the visitors travelled to the School…

> '…The L. and S.W.R. stopped the 10.40 train from
> Waterloo, and provided a reserve coach upon it for us.
> Carriages were stopped outside the gates, and we received
> our guests on the lawn… At 1.30 we moved to luncheon,
> and it was soon seen that there were very few places to spare.'

This great luncheon party was to be the principal event of the day, with 190 guests joining the Revd and Mrs Charles Wickham and the School in a huge tent erected on the Barley Field – where the all weather pitch would be sited some 95 years later.

To imbue the proceedings with a festive and patriotic air, the Band of the Hampshire Regiment had been engaged for the afternoon.

The Twyfordian rather charmingly completes the story of the Centenary celebrations…

> '…After luncheon there were a few short speeches … and then as
> we left the luncheon tent the rain, which had held off since
> 11 o'clock, came on again, and a move was made to the house…
> The Band played in Upper School, and the tent dinner wagon
> was wheeled about with ices and strawberries and cream…We can
> only hope that our O.T. guests were forgetting the rain in their
> vain search for their own names on desks, and in the interest of
> meetings and memories…Four o'clock brought more cricket, and
> tea in the big tent again; and then good byes and trains to catch,
> and Centenary Day was over.'

In 1910, after 23 years as Headmaster, Charles Wickham, although not old, announced his impending retirement. Mr Wickham's decision to retire was probably hastened by the fact that his wife, Flora, was not strong, and may have been finding that school life was becoming too great a burden for her. C.T.W. also suffered from increasingly poor health and within a few years was completely crippled by rheumatoid arthritis. Flora was to die suddenly only one year after Charles had retired. She was a gentle soul, who was particularly good with boys who were ill. She was a considerable expert on church needlework, and the white, red and violet altar hangings in the Chapel made by her remain as a fitting memorial to this day. She shared a great love of gardens with Charles Wickham and together they created a delightful cottage garden just to the south of The Cottage: sadly, this finally disappeared during the exacting years of the Second World War. Today, cars park where once flowers flourished.

The Sick House Garden c1905

The Cottage, at the entrance to the School, was known and used as the Sick House in the early years of the last century. Its garden was created by Charles and Flora Wickham, both of whom much enjoyed gardening. The summer-house is now a maintenance store.

At the School the Edwardian era passed smoothly. In the outside world there were many innovations and events to catch a boy's imagination: the first mass-produced car – the Model T Ford – took to the roads; the first aeroplanes took to the air; and perhaps of more immediate interest to children, the newly-invented ice cream cone took to the streets. It was also the age of polar exploration, and this was to touch Twyford in a small way. Shortly before the School held its centenary celebrations in 1909, Robert E. Peary had reached the North Pole, and the following year Captain Scott asked Twyford School (amongst others) for help in preparing for his Antarctic expedition.

Flora Wickham
(1863-1911)
Flora was the wife of the Revd C.T. Wickham. She died, aged 48, one year after her husband's retirement.

In early 1910, as Mr Wickham pondered retirement, elsewhere a great venture, which became the stuff of legend, was getting underway. Captain Robert Falcon Scott, Royal Navy, was planning his ill-starred expedition to the South Pole. As part of his preparation he needed to raise funds: he therefore wrote to some public and preparatory schools with an interesting sponsorship proposal. This extract from *The Twyfordian* of April 1910 tells us more:

'*Capt. Scott, the Antarctic explorer, sent us a circular at the beginning of the Term, asking the boys of England to subscribe to the outfit of the expedition for which he is now preparing. We sent him £4 5s. 6d., which, we understand, is sufficient to provide two sleeping bags, or a dog and a half. We expressed a hope that it might be spent on sleeping bags. As the bags are to be marked with the names of the schools which provide them, we hope that "Twyford" may keep somebody warm at the South Pole. If Commander Peary arrives at the same moment from the opposite direction there will probably be a pillow fight.*'

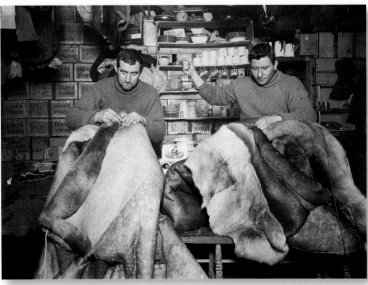

Repairing Sleeping Bags

Petty Officers Crean and Evans repairing their reindeer-skin sleeping bags during the Antarctic winter in May 1911 – was one of them marked 'Twyford'? Evans later died with Scott on the return journey from the South Pole.

The Final Journey

Evans, Oates, Wilson and Scott, in a photograph taken by Bowers, are on the Plateau having set out on the final leg of their journey to the South Pole. All perished 12 weeks later, on their return journey from the Pole where they had found that Amundsen had beaten them to it.

Some time after his retirement as Headmaster and before he became incapacitated, Charles Wickham came back to teach Set B and decided that he would like to do more to improve Upper School. As a result he offered to pay for its extension northwards to provide the space for the stage as we know it – and the installation upon it, in 1913, of a small, hydraulically blown organ built by W.J. Burton – all in memory of his wife, Flora. The hydraulic pump was remarkably advanced for its day, but in later years become notorious for its inability to generate a constant supply of air. Finally, in 1969, after 56 years on stage, the organ made its exit on being sold to a girls' school.

In order to extend Upper School to accommodate the stage, the north wall was removed. The 'backcourts' which had been on the other side of this wall were demolished and rebuilt (still as earth closets) on the outside of the new wall of the stage, where the boys' 'backcourts' are today. There had been an arched Georgian window in the original north end wall of Upper School. This was kept and then resited in the small classroom, adjacent to the stage, when it was built in the early 1920s.

The School's architect, the previously mentioned Herbert Kitchin, designed the whole project.

Upper School Fireplace after 1906

Note the chairs beside the fireplace, and the pictures above it: they, and much of the other furniture in Upper School, can be seen in the School to this day. The pictures are of 'A Twyfordian 1830', 'Boys at Play – 1848', and 'The Revd James Gover Bedford'.

Upper School c1913

This picture was taken soon after the stage extension and organ were added. Upper School was fairly austere. The floorboards were bare, although there is wallpaper to be seen above the panelling. There are gas lamps around the hall, but, even so, it must have been very gloomy on winter evenings.

Around this time, a new face was about to appear at Twyford, one which would have a profound influence on the School as proprietor and Headmaster. It was young Bob Wickham, who was C.T.W.'s nephew. In later life Bob Wickham said of C.T.W. that 'although he was always kind to the boys and was considerably beloved, he brought a stern element to his relationships, an element perhaps almost essential to good headmastership'. C.T.W. was pictured 'as having been carefree and dashing in his younger days, tall, athletic, a powerful hitter of a cricket ball and an over-daring wielder of a gun. He habitually over-charged his muzzle-loader, and in the end blew off the first finger of his right hand when it exploded.'

But in Bob Wickham's opinion, of all the earlier Heads, C.T.W. was perhaps the one who left the most lasting mark on the School: 'Charles Wickham's distinction lay in the tenacity and steadfastness which he proved by his determination to restore Twyford to prosperity even after the disasters of the diphtheria epidemic. No man could have been better equipped to do so.' Within the village of Twyford, he commanded the deference due to a feudal lord, and in 1928 it was there that, at the age of 66, C.T.W. died.

Newport Market Army Training School Visit 1910

The Newport Market Army Training School, later known as the Newport Market Army Bands School, was established in London in Victorian times to train homeless and destitute boys to become band boys in the Army. Twyford had a long-lasting liaison with this school, which paid an annual visit in the years before and after the First World War.

The usual programme was for the visitors to have a bathe in the river, followed by games, and lunch in the Parish Hall. In the afternoon there would be cricket matches at the School and entertainment by their band followed by chapel and tea. At the end of the day, the visitors would march to Shawford station with the band playing. This picture shows the band playing – perhaps as they are about to leave at the end of the visit – on 15 June 1910 when 86 boys visited Twyford.

In later years, as needs changed, the Newport Army Market Training School was merged with the charity now known as 'The Shaftesbury Homes and Arethusa'. This charity similarly supports young people in need or in care.

When Charles Wickham retired in 1910 he was succeeded by H.C. McDonell, an Old Twyfordian, who had joined the staff as an assistant master five years earlier. McDonell was to be the Headmaster for the next 27 years.

Bob Wickham, who arrived at the School as a pupil in April 1914, has left us a vivid picture of what he saw and experienced at that time. He spent his first night as a pupil in Great Work Room in the bed next to the door. The dormitories had board flooring and no central heating (much as they were until 1982!). There was a row of wash basins down the centre of the room which were filled each morning with tepid water in which the boys would, after a fashion, wash. Physical conditions were spartan – with cold baths every day, primitive lighting and heating, and earth closet sanitation. Indeed the early morning routine was pretty spartan too. The School bell rang at 7.45am. Each boy would jump out of bed, say his prayers, have a cold bath, read the Bible for ten minutes (known as 'Bibles'), run round the Playground with the Headmaster, shake his hand, and only then have breakfast. Breakfast consisted of porridge and a second course, and bread and marmalade when, later, the rather austere rations of the Great War permitted.

After breakfast there was a break for half an hour during which boys learnt by heart Latin or Greek grammar (known as 'rep'). The main day then started with Chapel and a double period of Latin followed by other subjects, including Greek. There were organised games on five afternoons a week. Then, as today, after 'bevers', lessons would continue, covering subjects considered less important than Latin and Greek – Mathematics, French, English Literature, History and Geography. School hours were long and lacked variety, whilst out-of-school activities were rather limited because the Headmaster felt that nothing should detract from organised games.

The sixth day provided time for hair-cutting, scouting, and other activities. Punishments were severe and corporal punishment, in Bob Wickham's opinion, was used far too frequently – both by the Headmaster, and even (with the Headmaster's permission) by senior boys who used a 'long-handled fives bat' for official beatings in the gym.

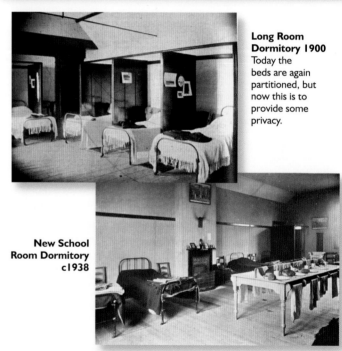

Long Room Dormitory 1900
Today the beds are again partitioned, but now this is to provide some privacy.

New School Room Dormitory c1938

This dormitory looked exactly the same for much of the first half of the 20th century. Indeed, apart from the removal of the washstands, and the addition of some modern embellishments such as carpets and curtains, it remained the same for the whole century. By 1938, the partitions erected in earlier years had been removed, although the wall battens to which they were attached can still be seen in this picture. The wooden partitions had been to minimise the transmission of infections.

A fresh impetus has been given this term to our Swedish Drill by the weekly visits of Mr. S. Jennings, who has come down from London by a very early train each Monday morning in order to assist us. On several occasions, too, he has stayed on after lunch to take a Master's Class—a strictly private affair—wherein many long-forgotten joints and muscles have been roused to articulate activity.

The Twyfordian, December 1913

Swedish Drill 1908
This is taking place in the 'temporary' gym created by Charles Wickham c1905. It was finally demolished when the new Sports Hall was built in 1989.

The Swimming Bath 1914
The Swimming Bath was built in 1914 and remained almost unchanged until demolished prior to the building of the modern Pool on the same site in 1989.

THE TWYFORDIAN.

Vol. XX.   JULY, 1914.   No 2.

SCHOOL NOTES.

The Summer Term ends on Tuesday, July 28th, and the Autumn Term will begin on Thursday, September 17th.

The frontispiece this term gives a view of the Swimming Bath—from a photograph taken by Mr. Marsh—looking towards the deep end and shewing the spring board and diving stage. The size of the bath is 40 feet by 20 feet, and it holds about 27,000 gallons of water. We have been using it nearly every day this term, and have not ceased to wonder how we ever did without it, especially in the hot weather! More than 40 boys can now swim two lengths or more, whereas at the beginning of the term not more than 15 boys could do so.

There were, however, distractions to enliven the days and leaven the common grind. By 1910 the Boy Scout movement had been founded and a very active troop was established at the School. This was partly through the support of Capt. The Hon. Roland Philipps, MC, an Old Twyfordian, who was Scout Commissioner for North East London, and who, at the age of only 26, was to be tragically killed on the Somme in 1916. The Chapel Choir went on an annual outing to places such as the New Forest. On one afternoon in July 1914, an Old Twyfordian paid a visit in an aeroplane, which at that time was an event indeed, as was the wireless telegraphy link set up by Mr Marsh between Mallard's Close (where he lived) and the School. Out in the Playground the boys played 'Kick the Block', a game of modified Hide and Seek.

Chatterbox
This well-loved annual was a popular staple of children's reading from 1866-1930 so must have been well-known to Twyford boys. The publication was founded by the Revd J. Erskine Clarke, who in 1875, became an Honorary Canon of Winchester.

H.C. McDonell
Headmaster and county cricketer

All in all, School life proceeded smoothly through Harold McDonell's first three years as Headmaster. *The Twyfordian,* in 1913, records that alterations were being made to the levels of parts of the games fields, and reports the deaths of Canon Francis Lear who had left Twyford in 1836 and of George Ricketts, a civilian hero of the Indian Mutiny of 1857. But probably of greater importance to the boys of the time was the Football 1st XI's recent defeat of West Downs, 6–1.

However, unbeknown to the little community that was Twyford School – masters and boys, domestic staff and gardeners – the immediate future was dark, very dark indeed.

Scout Camp 1914
In 1914 the Scout camp was held at Twyford on the Barley Field. In the above photograph the Swimming Bath building can be seen in the background. On the right the scouts are making early morning cocoa.

Summer Days in 1913

Empire Day, May 24th, was celebrated in the usual manner. We all saluted the flag before breakfast, sang the National Anthem at morning chapel, and had a half holiday in the afternoon.

On June 9th we all had tea in the hay in the field below the cricket field. After tea the whole school, with the exception of a few hay-fever victims, spent a hot but happy half-hour trying to smother each other, and some imprudent masters, with the loose hay. We then adjourned to the Itchen for a welcome and most necessary bathe. We might mention here that Mr. Wickham does not grow his hay simply and solely for the "hay-rag!"

The Twyfordian, July 1913

A Royal Aircraft Factory biplane (Type BE2a) similar to the one which came to Twyford in 1914, piloted by Old Twyfordian D.S. Lewis.

Mr. Marsh has again been kind enough to give short scientific lectures to some of the Upper School on Thursday evenings. One of these lectures was on the subject of "Wireless Telegraphy," and in the course of it wireless messages were sent from the IV. Form classroom to the Library. Mr. Marsh has himself fitted up a wireless installation at Mallard's Close, where it is possible to receive messages from Paris, North Germany, Poldhu, and other important stations. We understand that he has also permission from the Government to send messages to his friends in the neighbourhood!

The Twyfordian, December 1913

On coming out of School we all hurried into the field beyond Mallard's Close to see our old friend D. S. Lewis (O. T. 1895) of the Royal Flying Corps, who had flown over from Netheravon, near Salisbury, on the Army Biplane No. 336, to the camp at Cheriton, and paid us literally a "flying visit" on his way back. Some of us had never before seen a real live aeroplane at close quarters, and when we actually touched the wings we felt that we could now die happy! Mr. Lewis left again about 6.0 p.m. amid the cheers of the whole assembled population of Twyford.

The Twyfordian, July 1914

Lt Col D. S. Lewis, Royal Engineers (attached to the Royal Flying Corps) was to lose his life in 1916 (see page 61).

In recent years we have often been saddened by the news of deaths of, or severe injuries suffered by, young people serving in Iraq and Afghanistan. Similarly, from 1914 there were four years of misery and carnage that resulted in the deaths of 80 Old Twyfordians and staff, and the wounding of 116 (of whom 16 were later killed in action). Maybe upper lips were a little stiffer in those days of more frequent conflict abroad: the Crimea, West Africa, Afghanistan, China, South Africa, and so on, but the ceaseless reports of the loss of young men who had probably only just left their public schools before going to France, Gallipoli or Mesopotamia, must have been unutterably depressing and cause for many sad announcements and commemorations in the Chapel.

Some graphic reports were sent back from various fronts to the editor of *The Twyfordian*, and many remarkable citations for gallantry awards were published, where the formal words must mask the true horror of what had been going on. There is, in the School archives, a Book of Remembrance, published privately by Alfred Pope, Esq., FSA, JP, of Dorchester, with a foreword by Thomas Hardy, OM. It contains details of the war service of each of Alfred Pope's eleven sons. Seven of the boys were Old Twyfordians of whom two were killed. Two other sons and one son-in-law also perished. Three daughters became nurses.

Strangely, however, *The Twyfordian* – very much a serious document of record in those days – did not mention the actual outbreak of hostilities in 1914. The declaration of war had occurred during the summer holidays and many people confidently expected it to be 'over by Christmas'. In the December 1914 edition, however, it was at least reported that two masters – Messrs Bull and Cowland – had been called up for military service.

Of course the War was not 'over by Christmas' 1914, and for the next four years *The Twyfordian* trod a sensitive and often sad path between the listing of cricket scores and descriptions of School concerts, and the awful termly reports of the increasing numbers of dead, wounded and missing – punctuated by notifications of the awards of DSOs, MCs and very many Mentions in Despatches.

Casualties must often have been individually known to the Headmaster, Harold McDonell, from his time at the School as pupil, assistant master and Headmaster. Most of them – and their parents – will also have been clear in the memory of Charles Wickham, still working at the School as an assistant to McDonell.

Life at the School, during the four years of war, carried on nearly as normal. With most of the younger staff called up for service in the Army, older and medically unfit men filled their places very effectively, although the supervision of games must have been harder to organise.

Charles Wickham would certainly have remembered the boys who feature in this sad but all too typical story…

This picture taken c1899 shows Headmaster Charles Wickham with young Monk (*top left*) and young Hain (*bottom right*).

In January 1897, as the School assembled at Copthorne in Sussex for its year of enforced exile whilst the drains were reconstructed back at Twyford, a new boy, John Monk, joined Form III. At Easter another new boy, Edward Hain, arrived and was placed in the same form. They then went through the School together.

There are glimpses of them in the *Twyfordians* of the day, particularly in their last year when they took part in theatricals, and both played cricket for the School. Hain was Captain of the XI and Monk did well. Hain also won the Upper VI Classical Prize before going on to Winchester in September 1901: John Monk went to Malvern at the same time.

Later, after all too few years of young adulthood, they were, like most of their contemporaries, swept into the savagery that began in 1914.

Before the following year came to a close, Edward Hain, a Captain in the Royal 1st Devon Yeomanry, had been killed, and John Monk, likewise a Captain, but serving in the 1st Worcestershire Regt., had been wounded. Monk was later twice awarded the Military Cross and was Mentioned in Despatches. He survived the War itself but died in Khartoum in October 1920 'of illness contracted during military service in France'.

Another boy, Donald S. Lewis, was a year ahead of Monk and Hain. He was a good sportsman and won the Longley Cup, played cricket for the School and was Captain of the football team. He also played 'Puss in Boots' in a wax-work exhibition. In 1914 Lieutenant Lewis, Royal Engineers, flew a biplane to Twyford (*see page 59*), but two years later was killed in action in Belgium.

Edward Hain
Captain, Royal 1st Devon Yeomanry. He was killed in action at Gallipoli on 11 November 1915 in his 29th year.

John Monk
Captain, 1st Worcestershire Regt. He was wounded in 1915, awarded the Military Cross and Bar, 1916 and 1917, and Mentioned in Despatches, 1918. He died in Khartoum in 1920.

Donald Lewis

Photographed at Twyford in 1899 as winner of the Longley Cup.

As Lt Col D.S. Lewis, Royal Engineers (attached to the Royal Flying Corps), he was awarded the DSO and MC. He was killed in action in Belgium in 1916, aged 30.

In September 1914, he and his crew used airborne radio for the first time in warfare when directing an artillery shoot from the air during the First Battle of the Aisne.

It was Donald Lewis who had paid the 'flying visit' to Twyford in 1914.

Early in 1915 a large military camp was established at Hazeley Down, just over a mile east of the School. Here many of the newly-raised London battalions received their final training before being marched along the Hazeley Road, through Twyford village to Shawford and on to Southampton. From there they were shipped to northern France for the mud and shells of the trenches. From time to time Old Twyfordian platoon and company commanders will have been among them – and young Twyfordians at the School will have been aware of those marching hundreds. Wayside crosses of commemoration for these men can still be seen at Hazeley Down and on the hill above Shawford railway station.

At the School itself, the purchase of sufficient nutritious food for the boys began to be a continuing headache

Hazeley Road, Twyford.

Soldiers walking along Hazeley Road in 1915

for the Headmaster and his sister, Miss McDonell. By late 1916 German submarines had achieved a high level of success in sinking Allied merchant ships and many types of food were scarce: however, the School excelled in the production of vegetables, to the extent that its surplus crops were added to those of other gardens in the village and sent to help feed the Fleet.

The boys not only grew vegetables but did much of the maintenance work required in the games fields and in the gardens. This was essential because when an under-gardener, young Bert Stratton,

reached call-up age in early 1918 he was the ninth School gardener to be recruited for military service.

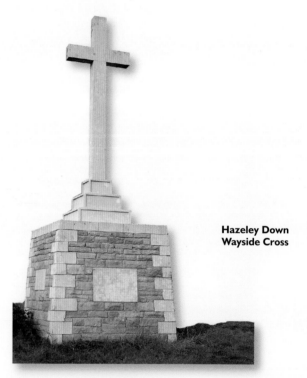

Hazeley Down Wayside Cross

The Twyfordian was published each term throughout the First World War and in every issue there was a Roll of Honour: this listed Old Twyfordians who had been reported as killed, wounded, or taken prisoner since the previous issue. Awards and decorations were also shown and sometimes citations or obituaries were printed.

The example of such a Roll of Honour (*page 63*) is one of the shortest of the 13 or so covering the period of the War.

One of the major concerns of the Second World War – that of possible random bombing by German aircraft which had failed to find their Portsmouth or Southampton targets – was not such a problem in the First World War. Bombing raids by German aircraft and Zeppelins (airships) became common from 1915 onwards, but they tended to attack London and the Midlands more than Hampshire, and it was not until 1916 that a black-out system was enforced in the area – and anyway, the standard of lighting at the School, as normally permitted by the Headmaster and his sister, was, to say the least, discreet and unlikely to catch the eye of a Zeppelin crew.

In early 1917 the boys had an opportunity to make another contribution to the war effort by adding, to their vegetable production, the sorting of thousands of personal record cards for the local Recruiting Officer. This was done in Upper School – and displays an unexpected but welcome show of confidence by that official.

The Roll of Honour (*right*) is from *The Twyfordian, December 1916*. The date given is the year the named person joined the School.

ROLL OF HONOUR (since July 1916)

Accidentally Injured
Flight-Commander A.R. Arnold, R.N.A.S. 1905

Killed in Action or Died of Wounds
Second-Lieut. W.C. Trimmer, Oxford and Bucks Light Infantry 1906
Lieut. R.J.A. Bowles, Welch Fusiliers 1901
Lieut. E.R. Cholmeley, West Yorkshire Regiment 1903
Lieut. T.E.O. Chamberlayne, R.F.A. 1904
Second-Lieut. H.T.T. Gore-Browne, King's Own Rifles......................... 1896
Second-Lieut. W.T. Hichens, Duke of Cornwall's Light Infantry 1904
Second-Lieut. W.N. Young, Royal Scots Fusiliers 1907
Lieut. P.P. Pope, 3rd Welsh Regiment.. 1893
Second-Lieut. N. Butler, Irish Guards 1900

Died in England
Major A.J. Pell, Suffolk Regiment 1873

Wounded
Second-Lieut. D.W. Suthery, Seaforth Highlanders 1907
Second-Lieut. G.H. Greenwell, Oxford and Bucks Light Infantry.............. 1891
Second-Lieut. C.G. Cardew, R.E. 1905
Second-Lieut. W.A. Lister, King's Royal Rifles 1906
Major F.H. Gunner, D.S.O., South Staffordshire Regiment 1897
Second-Lieut. B.H. Sumner, King's Royal Rifles................................. 1902

Prisoner of War
Second-Lieut. G.B. Slater, London Regiment 1903

Mentioned in "Jutland" Despatches
Commodore E.E. Alexander-Sinclair, C.B., M.V.O., A.D.C., who first gained touch with the enemy forces, would have been recommended for an honour had he not so recently received the C.B...................................... 1876

Military Cross
Lieut. W.G. Gisborne, 9th Lancers.. 1904
Lieut. William Guy Gisborne, Lancers. He assisted his Senior Officer in rallying a number of Infantry, who had lost their officers and were retiring. They led them forward and consolidated a position under fire. Later, when his Senior Officer was wounded, he brought him in under heavy rifle and machine gun-fire...

Mentioned in Despatches
Major-Gen. R.G. Egerton, C.B., Indian Army 1869
Major-Gen. G.V. Kemball, C.B., D.S.O., Indian Army............................ 1871
Lieut. R.C.H. Woodhouse (died of wounds), 56th Punjabi Rifles 1901
Major (temp. Lieut.-Col.) G.V. Clarke, D.S.O., Yeomanry 1886

French Decoration – Croix de Guerre
Captain and Brevet Major A.C. Johnston, M.C., Worcester Regt............... 1895

The Twyfordian in 1917 records the death of the old mare which had pulled the grass mower across the games fields for many years – and the wounding in action of the School's only holder of the Victoria Cross: Lieut Gen Sir Walter Congreve, VC, KCB, MVO. It was not only the young, junior officers who were at risk.

The linking of such pieces of news may seem inappropriate. It was, however, the way that the School could record connections with its past, honour Twyfordians struggling with the awful present – and encourage its boys to look forward to their futures by reporting their concerts, their cricket scores and their academic successes.

∾

The Twyfordian also gives an account of the lives of two Old Twyfordians to whom fate had dealt very different hands. Both died within two weeks of Armistice Day, 11 November 1918, having served their country with distinction:

Robert Biddulph had been at Twyford in the 1840s and joined the Royal Artillery as a Second Lieutenant in 1853. He served in the Crimean War, had been involved in both the relief of Lucknow during the Indian Mutiny and in the China war of 1861. He died, aged 83, after a long and distinguished career.

Desmond Cancellor left Twyford in 1912. Six years later, when serving as a Second Lieutenant in the Hampshire Regiment in northern France, he died on active service at the age of 20, a few days before the war ended.

∾

Robert Biddulph

The Twyfordian, December 1918, reported: 'On Monday, November 18th, there passed away one of the oldest and most distinguished Twyfordians.' General Sir Robert Biddulph GCB, GCMG, had died at the age of 83. After joining the Royal Artillery in 1853, service overseas was followed by four years as Military Secretary to the Commander in Chief, Madras. Later he was Private Secretary to the Secretary of State for War, and subsequently High Commissioner and Commander in Chief, Cyprus. He must have done well, for after this appointment he was promoted Major General and awarded the GCMG.

Thereafter he served in other military appointments including Quartermaster General, and finally as Governor of Gibraltar, from which he retired in 1902. During his service, he found time to marry the daughter of the rector of Chilbolton and have ten children. He died at home in London and was buried at Woolwich. After the interment the customary volleys were fired by a firing party of the Royal Artillery, who had escorted the gun carriage and funeral procession with arms reversed; the trumpeters of the Royal Artillery sounded the 'Last Post'.

Desmond Cancellor

Desmond Cancellor went to Radley from Twyford in 1912. Although destined for Oxford, he left Radley to commence military training in 1916, and the following year was commissioned as a Second Lieutenant in the Hampshire Regiment and went to France. He was wounded twice in the next few weeks and returned to England to spend several months in hospital. Whilst convalescing he wrote a novel – *Young England* – under the pseudonym 'Douglas Strong'. He returned to France in September 1918 only two months before the end of the war.

The Battalion to which he was attached suffered many casualties during a sustained period of fighting, leaving Lieutenant Cancellor in command of his Company. Whilst successfully engaged in silencing a machine-gun position, he was mortally wounded. His body was carried back to the French village of Haspres, where it was buried. The obituary in *The Twyfordian* described it as 'pathetically fitting that this should be his last resting place', as, a few days earlier, Cancellor had picked up and carried to safety from that village a child who had been wounded in the head by German shelling. After Cancellor's death, his Colonel wrote, in a letter to his mother, that 'He was simply magnificent. He died a great death, loved by all with whom he came in contact.'

In September 1918, there was a huge Allied offensive, launched in northern France and Belgium, responding to a violent but ultimately unsuccessful one mounted by the Germans that spring. Second Lieutenant Desmond Cancellor captured a sense of what it was like in a sketch he wrote 'somewhere in France in October 1918':

'"Boom – Boom – Boom!" The high-pitched shriek of a shell, a crash – and a barrage had dropped. Every nerve was taut. The crouching men gripped their rifles. Heads well down. Flare after flare went up. The whole world seemed a chaos of noise and light and smoke.

'A shell dropped thirty yards short of them. Then another fifteen yards behind them. The subaltern began to shiver. He thanked God that it was too dark for the men to see. What should he do? Move forward or keep the men where they were?

'"Whew!" that one was close. A shower of earth pattered down on their tin hats. Why the devil wouldn't the firing stop?

'Ah! There were their own guns beginning, that was better. "Wruf!" The hot blast of a shell fanned the subaltern's face. He crouched lower, hugging the ground. A machine gun had started its rat-tat-tat… they were damnably isolated out here, with the wire behind them and the Boche in front.'

On 24 October 1918 Cancellor won the Military Cross 'for most conspicuous gallantry and fearless leadership'. A week later he was killed in action, a few days before the Armistice.

On that first Armistice Day, Twyford School, recently in the grip of an epidemic of influenza, was almost empty. Most of the boys had been sent home, either healthy to protect them from risk, or unwell in order to recover. They came back to a peacetime school on 14 November.

On the great day itself, whilst Winchester celebrated the Armistice, *The Twyfordian* reported that at the School 'only a few tired or convalescent folk [were] about to do the cheering and the flag-waving. On receiving the news we at once hoisted the flag, and in the evening we had a brief thanksgiving service, attended by the entire household, in the School Chapel.'

Within a month of the momentous signing of the Armistice, *The Twyfordian* tells us that 'a circular letter [was] being sent round to Old Twyfordians with sketches of the Memorial Library which it is proposed to erect here in memory of Twyford's sacrifice in the Great War'.

Finally, as a footnote to the events of this historically significant term, the death was reported of Sir Hubert Parry, the great national musician and composer. He was 70 years of age and was one of the dwindling band of men who had been inspired as boys by the Revd G.W. Kitchin in the 1850s.

Armistice Day in Winchester 1918
A band is playing to cheerful crowds during a parade in the High Street. The distinctive town clock, which can still be seen today, stands at 11.50am.

King's Royal Rifle Corps Memorial
Winchester Cathedral
Sculptor John Tweed, 1922.
A number of Old Twyfordians served in the KRRC.

During the next two or three years the echoes of the Great War diminished. *The Twyfordian* reported a final death and a last batch of awards and decorations. It also gave progress reports on the plans for the Memorial Library and the receipt of a vast number of monetary subscriptions towards its cost from Old Twyfordians, parents and other friends of the School.

Amongst other items of news was a report of the death of Mrs Emma Bedford, aged 100. She was the second wife of the Revd J.G. Bedford (Headmaster 1815-1833) and had, in 1902, given the School the portrait of Mr Bedford that has already been mentioned.

It was also noted that the Scout troop's equipment had been given away to the Winchester HQ troop. This seems strange for, throughout the Great War, Twyford School's troop had been exceptionally successful and active: as we have seen, several enjoyable camps had been held and, in 1915, the Scouts had created a 6-hole golf course in the School grounds.

The Memorial Library

At last, in January 1923, the Memorial Library, which had been designed by architect Herbert Kitchin, was formally opened for use. Although some of the fine oak interior fittings had still to be completed, a beautiful leather-bound book with vellum pages had been made. This contained an illuminated Roll of Honour, listing those from the School – former boys and staff – who had served, and died, in the Great War. This is still on display with the pages being turned periodically.

The Memorial Library soon after construction and (*below*) the cartouche above the bookcase.

Over 280 individuals and couples were listed as subscribers to the cost of building the Library and, as a consequence, re-laying 'Court' in its present position.

In addition to the Memorial Library, a carved wood memorial board was placed at the west end of the Chapel. Doubtless, it was optimistically hoped that the Great War of 1914 to 1918 would prove to have been the war to end all wars: that schools would never again have to list tragic losses of this nature.

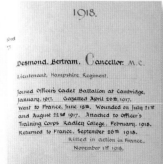

By the time H.C. McDonell had guided the School through the Great War and its aftermath, he was almost half way through his headship. Harold McDonell, who was not to marry until after his retirement from Twyford many years later, ran the School, assisted by his spinster sister, Daisy (*right*), who kept house for him. Daisy, generally dressed in black and nearly always wearing a hat, had a formal manner and, now and again, a wintry smile. (This picture of her, and one of the Headmaster, were given to boys on leaving the School.) McDonell himself had a distinguished scholastic and sporting career. After success as a boy at Twyford, he had built upon it at Winchester and then went on to Cambridge where he was a Scholar of Corpus Christi College, a cricket blue and Captain of golf. He played cricket for Surrey, and regularly for Hampshire which he captained on several occasions in 1914 and 1921.

As Headmaster of Twyford, McDonell proved to be intensely conservative, not welcoming educational change or technical innovations. To the end of their time at the School, the McDonells distrusted electricity – Daisy assuring the young Bob Wickham that it 'was so dangerous when it went round the corners'. Despite this innate conservatism, for much of Harold McDonell's time the School prospered and his reign was marked by a number of additions to the School and its amenities. Of these, there were two important developments in his early years, fortunately completed before the onset of war in August 1914. A new games field, called 'New Ground', was created by the levelling of the land in the south-east corner of the grounds, below what is now the all weather pitch. The north side was terraced for spectators, and one of Bob Wickham's earliest memories was of the boys being formed up in long lines – as was repeated when the cricket ground in front of the main house was being levelled in 1989 – to remove the unwanted flints which continually worked their way to the surface.

In 1914 a covered Swimming Bath had been built, and it was used until 1989 when the modern one was built on the same site. The 1914 pool was heated by a large high pressure coal-fired steam boiler which noisily blew steam through the water. Subsequently the section of the River Itchen where the boys had learnt to swim soon silted up as it was no longer being used.

Two other changes were made in the early 1920s. A classroom was built adjacent to the Upper School stage. It incorporated the arched Georgian window which had been removed and preserved when the stage had been added a decade earlier. In the grounds, a thatched shelter, designed by Herbert Kitchin, was built between the Barley Field and New Ground, and a sunken cricket net site was dug: this was used until the main cricket pitch was created in 1989. By a happy coincidence the modern 1st XI cricket square lies about eight feet above the site of the original cricket nets.

The Thatched Shelter – then known as the 'Beehive' – as it was in 1928.

Mallard's Close 1910

Mallard's Close was built in the late 1880s for Mr H.C. Strahan, Headmaster in Partnership with the Revd C.T. Wickham from 1890-1896. Strahan, however, moved into what is now known as The Cottage. Mallard's Close was thereafter used mainly as staff accommodation for the next 100 years before being sold in 1986 to fund the first batch of new classrooms.

The sole occupant from 1910-1933 was Mr G.R. Marsh, the 'Mr Chips' of Twyford, who loved everything mechanical and scientific. Bob Wickham recalled the boys' Sunday invitations to Mallard's Close: 'The Mallard's Close teas were little less than an introduction to fairyland for boys. The visit to the greenhouse where passion fruit and every kind of odd and exotic plant was grown. The pianola in the drawing room, caterpillars of all sorts crawling under bell-jars, Wimshurst machines which often would not work; a vast tea with the inevitable "poison", a particularly fearsomely decorated cake; puzzles to solve, microscopes to look through, a room completely devoted to swinging pendulums which drew elaborate designs; the dark room and chemical laboratory where one was always invited to smell "the worst smell in the world".'

The School Song *(above)* was printed in *The Twyfordian* in 1915. The words were written by C.T. Wickham and the music was composed by the School's Head of Music, W. S. Cowland.

The Upper School stage and organ *(right)* were given by C.T. Wickham in memory of his wife, Flora, as commemorated on a brass plaque in Upper School (see *page 54*).

McDonell was a man of moods who lived on his nerves and appeared stern and formidable to the boys. In everything he sought the highest standards, and he praised sparingly. However, one Old Boy of pre-First World War days wrote that 'A word of praise from him to us boys was like champagne and quickly went to our heads'. Michael Audland, another Old Twyfordian who was a pupil of McDonell a quarter of a century later, recalled that 'Failures in Doni's class might well be followed by a visit to his study for a beating. He did have a very short fuse but, on the other side, fear did add speed to the learning wings!'

It was a severe era, and the boys of those days, now elderly men, found it austere. One recalled the boiled egg which each boy was allowed to have for breakfast on the last day of term; another, the canes which Mr McDonell kept on his desk. They also remember the old, rusting German machine gun in the bushes which the boys used as a plaything.

The older H.C. McDonell

Michael Audland's Recollections

Michael Audland recalled his early days at Twyford, which he joined in 1932:

'I suppose that in 1932 the School was still locked firmly into the Edwardian era. I arrived on my first day in my knickerbocker suit, which I detested, my Eton collar which I equally disliked and my regulation cap. I must have looked rather like my father did in about 1905. I am not at all sure that my parents had ever seen the School before they set off for India in early 1930. Had they done so, would they have sent me? Probably yes, as my Mother had had a blissful childhood in a large house in the heyday of the Edwardian era; this experience endowed her with values which remained with her for the rest of her life; they were somewhat uncomfortable for her children at times. My aunt who did bring me to the School on my first day told me years later that she was horrified.

'At least my Mother was more than a match for Mr McDonell. In December 1932 my parents returned on leave to Southampton and got a chauffeur driven car to take them to the School in order to see their son after nearly three years of being apart. Mr McDonell would not allow this as it was not an official Leave Out Day but he had met his match; my Mother stood firm and I was produced. Incidentally, a month before, on the occasion of my 9th birthday, my Grandmother sent me three cakes; they were opened in my presence and then returned to her! There would have been enough for every boy to have a slice.'

◆～◎

Dr A.R.H. Worssam's Recollections

Dr A.R.H. Worssam, Old Twyfordian (1933-1938), has many memories of those days:

'I was at Twyford just before the war, and although it was bitterly cold and we were always hungry, I enjoyed most of my time; and the teaching was good and very concentrated…We wore Eton collars, got caned from time to time and proudly compared our stripes in the dormitory – [there was] only gas light in much of the School. The main lavatories were a row of earth closets with half doors; and Fred, the ex-service, lame bell-ringer and shoe cleaner, used to empty them, each in turn, from outside. Cricket, and to a lesser degree football, was a religion.

'…We spent much of the time catching and mounting butterflies, and kept grass snakes, or perhaps slow worms, in shoe boxes, and hunting for owl pellets in the large trees on the edge of the playing fields…McDonell was a man of wide interests. We were all taught to swim, including several lengths with our clothes on, we were taken for wonderful walks in the water meadows, and he read to us in front of the fire in his study on Sunday evenings…Unusual and interesting lecturers came to Twyford, including a deep sea diver who appeared in a full diver's suit and then sang sea shanties. Others came and recited Kipling.

'I loved chapel, with rousing hymns, especially on Remembrance Sunday, and at the end of the term the same lesson "Let us now praise famous men, and our fathers that begat us…"…I was a "non-singer" and pumped the organ instead. Once, for a dare, I let it run out of air so it died with a long sigh. I may well have been beaten'.

The Pavilion, pictured here in 1903, was situated near the eastern end of the ha-ha, and was used throughout most of the 20th century.

Orchard Cottage 1913. This cottage was once the home of the School butler – referred to as 'King', not 'Mr King' – who served the top table at meal times until he left in 1938. Latterly it was the home of Head Groundsman, Ted Unsworth, until its demolition in 1987. His daughter, Phyllis Justice, a present member of the domestic staff, spent her childhood in this house. The cottage was sited on what is now the eastern courtyard in front of the Sports Hall.

Mr McDonell could relax, but seldom did so, except when he was playing games. From the ha-ha he would take on the whole School in a snowball fight, proving to be a good-tempered and formidable opponent. His readings on Sunday evenings were usually from Dickens or Scott and he was an artist in assuming the character he was reading.

McDonell's right hand man on the non-academic front was Charles Oxenbury, known as 'Chauce'. Chauce had first come to the School as Latham Wickham's coachman, and in 1889, following Mr Wickham's retirement, became the bell-ringer, boot cleaner, lamp-lighter, and general factotum. He lived with his family in a cottage over the stables (where Stablecross, the Pre-Prep nursery, now stands), and knew everyone and every nook and cranny of the buildings.

In Victorian times one of the School's ponies, when not being driven by Charles Wickham in a dog cart, pumped water from a well as already described. From the nearby boot room, Chauce would hurl a boot at the pony should it stop walking around the well. He also drove the cart to the village laundry each week, and took the old wagonette to the station at the end of term. In summer there would be expeditions to Longwood and elsewhere. Chauce finally retired in 1925 after 44 years of service. He died in 1940 at the age of 88, and now lies beneath a yew tree in Twyford churchyard.

∾

The Cart

This cart was used for many years in the first part of the 20th century to take children to and from Shawford station – and the boys' washing to Miss Hackshaw's laundry in Twyford village. In later years it was used by the boys as a plaything: in this 1973 picture a gang of boys led by J.S.B. Woolley, pull the cart across the Barley Field (where the all weather pitch now lies). The Thatched Shelter is in the top right corner of the picture.

Another plaything that some Old Boys recall is the machine gun – albeit an old rusting one – which was in the hedge in the background of this picture during the 1930s.

School Interior
These pictures show the School as it was for much of the first half of the 20th century.

Central Hall (c1898)
(*above*) and **The Main Staircase** (*right*) remained much the same until the 1970s when a fire partition was built around the staircase. This was removed in 2008 when modern electrical fire safety equipment was fitted instead.

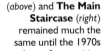

The Lower School (*left*) had been one of the first classrooms and later became, in turn, boys' dining room, library, and seniors' classroom. It is now the Boarders' Drawing Room. The wooden fire-surround, with the School motto carved across the top, is still in the same position today.

The Great Gale

'During the winter we had a succession of severe gales, which culminated in one of quite exceptional ferocity on the evening of Sunday, January 12th. Trees were blown down in all directions, roads were blocked and telephone wires torn down for miles round Winchester.

'At about 8.15 pm the big chimney stack on the road side of the kitchen and dining-hall was blown down, and crashed through the roof of the dining-hall itself, making a hole some ten to fifteen feet square. The whole mass of débris fell into the dining-hall, smashing several tables and benches, and cracking the main beam supporting the floor. Mercifully the floor just held, otherwise the whole mass would have been precipitated into the scullery below. Even as it was the damage was sufficiently serious, as our illustration shows, and a very brief examination by experts enabled them to decide that it would take at least three weeks, under favourable conditions, to render the kitchen and dining-hall usable again. So there was no alternative but to inform parents that it was necessary to prolong the holidays…On the whole the news was taken philosophically by all concerned.'

The Twyfordian, April 1930

H.C. Scott
H.C. Scott was a master at Twyford from 1897-1931 and an almost exact contemporary of George Marsh. The Boarders' Drawing Room was created in the earlier Lower School room in 1997 with a bequest from the estate of his widow.

G.R. Marsh 1909
George Marsh (*centre*) had been a boy at Twyford from 1885-1889 and was a master from 1898-1933

H arold McDonell was supported by a strong academic team many of whom, it turned out, were to be the backbone of the School for very many years to come.

H.C. Scott, a fine mathematician, and literary acrostic puzzle compiler of national standing, came in 1897 and left 34 years later. G.R. Marsh, an Old Twyfordian, arrived the following year and stayed for 35 years. He was a lover of all sorts of contraptions and things that would appeal to young boys, introducing them to many of the new inventions of the age such as phonographs, magic lanterns and wireless. As already mentioned, a visit to his house, Mallard's Close, on Sundays was a veritable treat for the boys.

The School had remained prosperous for many of the years of McDonell's headship but, from 1929 onwards, suffered a sharp decline in numbers. In 1910 when he became the Headmaster there were 69 boys, and by the late 1920s this had risen to the maximum capacity of 73. It was said that one term the School was doing so well that McDonell decided not to charge any school fees! However, the good times were not to last, and eight years later numbers had dropped to 37. As 50 boys were required to cover costs, clearly a crucial point had been reached. Doubtless the economic effects of the Great Depression had a damaging effect but parents anyway were beginning to look more critically at their children's schools, and Twyford's lack of creature comforts was a reflection of McDonell's austerity. Harold McDonell would not allow the gas-lighting used elsewhere in the School to be extended to the dormitories, and, although drains had been laid to the School lavatories – the 'backcourts' – after the diphtheria epidemic, McDonell retained the earth closet system rather than install water closets. The bricked up apertures at the rear of each lavatory pedestal were still visible until the 'backcourts' were rebuilt in the 1980s: it was through these apertures that the earth closets were serviced by the houseman. Despite these privations, however, Twyford boys achieved the top academic award to Winchester in each of McDonell's last two years, a notable achievement for a school of less than 40 pupils.

ob Wickham had inherited the School in 1928 on the death of his uncle, C.T. Wickham. He had gone on to Winchester from Twyford, and came down from Oxford with degrees in History and Theology. He was ordained and, in the same year that he inherited Twyford, joined the staff of Marlborough as a young teacher. By 1937 it was plain that, if the School were to survive, radical steps would have to be taken, and Harold McDonell offered his resignation. Thus, at the tender age of 32, the Revd R.G. Wickham took over as Headmaster, fulfilling his destiny. Mr McDonell and Daisy left the School that had been central to their lives for so many years, intending to live together in a house they had bought in Scotland. But, no sooner had he retired, than Harold announced his forthcoming marriage to a distant cousin, and Daisy went to live with her sister instead.

Bob Wickham faced many problems. He took over large premises with an established academic staff and the many others needed to run the School. As already mentioned, this required the fees from at least 50 boys to cover the costs, and at 37 the numbers were far short of that. Electric lighting was still not fully installed, the sanitation was

The Revd and Mrs R.G. Wickham c1950

medieval – drains which had been installed in 1897 following the diphtheria epidemic were for the most part not being used – and there were black beetles everywhere. The curriculum was in a similar state: it had been devised in 1894, twenty years before Bob Wickham had entered the School as a boy.

In addition to all the problems the Wickhams faced, there was an even greater imponderable. Despite high level political efforts to avoid conflict only 20 years after the terrible war of 1914-1918, it was clear that such efforts might be unsuccessful: any improvements that the new Headmaster might make could therefore be of limited value.

Nevertheless, Bob and his charming and capable wife, Betty, were young, cheerful, and much too light-hearted to let the daunting task ahead get them down. They were supported by good people both then and in future years. Miss Hunt, the Senior Matron, had come with them from Marlborough and, later, Miss Mary Pursey was to serve as Head Matron from 1947-1971. Mr Leslie Davies had joined the School as the French teacher in 1925. He was to stay for 25 years and was a great worker with an excellent memory. Major J.C. Bull, MC, a first class teacher of mathematics, arrived in 1905, the same year as Mr McDonell, and was to remain at Twyford for the next 56 years! As the Second Master, he was a highly experienced colleague, who in earlier days had taught the young Bob. Amongst the lively young teachers were Desmond Hill and Charles Mason. Desmond Hill was to lose his life while serving with Coastal Command during the Second World War. Charles Mason, of Shrewsbury, and Brasenose College, Oxford, who had joined the School in 1932, was in the Army during the war, and later became a wonderful Twyford character who was to serve the School for 52 years.

Long-Serving Staff

In the middle years of the twentieth century many staff, both academic and non-academic, served the School for much of their working lives and all would have been very familiar figures indeed to Major Bull and Mr Wickham. Maud Godwin was a much-loved and bustling parlour-maid for upwards of 40 years from the late 1920s, and members of the Stratton family were notable for their long and faithful service extending in total to over 100 years. Of particular note are Winnie Stratton, who came in 1921 and served on the domestic staff for over 35 years, and her brother Fred Stratton, who probably joined in 1912 and was the general factotum and handyman, around whom the School revolved thereafter for over 58 years. In his early years he had been a boot-boy who cleaned all the boys' shoes daily, and a gardener. Later he took over from Charles Oxenbury on his retirement. For many years he trimmed the large number of oil lamps around the School, and he rang the School bell so reliably that Twyford villagers were able to set their clocks by it. He did many a repair job with Bob Wickham, and was to be an invaluable asset during the Second World War.

In those happy pre-war days one of the favourite features of the Summer term had been the cricket match between the School 1st XI and what was called the 'Club and Ground', a mixed side of academic and domestic staff. The stars of the day were always Tom Oxford, cowman for 36 years, and Fred Stratton (with a runner because of his stiff leg), both of whom batted with great élan. The annual 'Club and Ground' match was to continue until 1983.

Major Bull and Mr Wickham passing the time of day

" TOM "
" WINNIE "   " THE MAJOR "   " FRED "
                                         "ARCHIE "

The 'Stalwarts'
Long-serving staff photographed in later years.
The group in this picture were to give a total of over 220 years of service.
(*rear L to R*) Tom Oxford (36 years), Fred Stratton (58 years),
(*front L to R*) Winnie Stratton (over 35 years), Major Bull (56 years),
Archie Stewart (37 years).

Gardens and Gardeners

For very many years the gardens were a large and important source of fruit and vegetables for the School. They covered much of the ground to the north of the old School buildings, now the site of the courtyards and most of the modern classrooms. Nestled amongst them was the Victorian gardeners' brick-built shed, a quiet and quaint reminder of the land's original use. Bob Wickham recalled 'the heavily side-whiskered gardeners in their billy-cock hats'. This building is adjacent to the newest classroom block, Saxon Court, and remains in use to this day.

The head gardener for many years was Dick Aslet who had joined the School in 1915. He was to be seen hard at work, always dressed in a stiff collar and a trilby hat. He was guided by nature, and planted potatoes at a particular phase of the moon, and dug them up at some other propitious time. He was not, however, very successful at forecasting requirements, and carloads of lettuce would be ferried to the local hospital because they had become ready for picking in the first week of the summer holidays. One of the assistant gardeners was Archie Stewart who joined

The Walled Garden
Although this picture of the walled garden looking north away from the School buildings was taken in 1983, the scene would have been familiar to many earlier generations.

the School in 1920. In addition to being a gardener, he was the only person who could handle the swimming pool boiler, and the ancient pony that was used for mowing. This toothless old pony worked very slowly, coming to a standstill when it needed a rest. But it did most of the School mowing, and its death during the Second World War ended the long line of ponies that had served the School since its early days.

Whilst adults attended to the business of growing food in the School's large gardens, the boys cultivated their own individual small gardens. The first mention of these gardens was in 1896, and they have been an on-going feature ever since. Prizes were awarded each summer for the best garden, and those who failed to keep a good garden could expect to receive a rap on the knuckles in *The Twyfordian*. Occasionally there were successes of such scale that they gained a mention in the School magazine: in 1925 one team of boys grew a sunflower which attained a height of just under ten feet.

Boys' Gardens
In this picture dated 1988 the boys' gardens were on the playing fields at the front of the School. Today they are in the walled garden.

As well as having a vegetable garden, the School had a small dairy farm which was in fields to the south of its grounds. It was to survive until 1978 and is described in more detail on page 89.

In 1939, the Summer term ended on Tuesday, 1 August. The boys went home, mostly unaware of the international tensions that were doubtless worrying their parents and Mr and Mrs Wickham. The boys who returned seven weeks later came back from a totally different world but, as far as they were concerned, to a largely unchanged School. Whilst they were on holiday the Second World War had broken out.

The previous year the threat of war had begun to produce staffing problems. Wartime copies of *The Twyfordian* make School life seem remarkably unaffected by the war, but Bob Wickham's recollections indicate just how much hard work was involved in keeping the School running smoothly, not to mention the great responsibility borne by him and Betty for the safety and well-being of their young charges.

Men of military age were called up, leaving gaps in academic and domestic staff. Throughout the war, teaching staff replacements were provided by women or men awaiting call-up, and the grounds staff was so depleted that the masters had to dig potatoes and mow grass as well as teach the boys.

Travelling and administration were difficult, and there were shortages of various kinds. It was hard to obtain clothing and shoes, stationery, and sports equipment such as balls and hockey sticks – the School's allocation was one stick

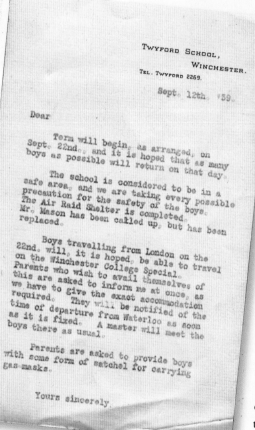

Twyford School,
Winchester.
Tel. Twyford 2269.

Sept. 12th '39.

Dear

Term will begin, as arranged, on Sept. 22nd, and it is hoped that as many boys as possible will return on that day.

The school is considered to be in a safe area, and we are taking every possible precaution for the safety of the boys. The Air Raid Shelter is completed. Mr. Mason has been called up, but has been replaced.

Boys travelling from London on the 22nd, will, it is hoped, be able to travel on the Winchester College Special. Parents who wish to avail themselves of this are asked to inform me at once, as we have to give the exact accommodation required. They will be notified of the time of departure from Waterloo as soon as it is fixed. A master will meet the boys there as usual.

Parents are asked to provide boys with some form of satchel for carrying gas-masks.

Yours sincerely,

per term. One Summer term Physical Training was done in bare feet owing to a shortage of PT shoes. However, although food was rationed, no one went hungry as they had in the First World War.

The number of boys slowly rose from 37 to the mid 40s which was as many as could be managed given the wartime problems.

Various air raid preparations were made at the onset of war. Every day Fred Stratton put up, and took down, 90 plywood black-out shutters on the windows, which would also provide protection against shattering glass. An air raid shelter was built entirely by School staff. It was in the style of a Nissen hut set four feet into the ground and covered with three feet of earth. It was sited in what later became the west courtyard. Bob Wickham, assisted by Fred Stratton, made timber bunks in which everyone was able to sleep. The whole School could be evacuated from dormitories to the air raid shelter in two and a half minutes. In 1940, during the Battle of Britain, the boys spent much time in the shelter. The alarms generally occurred between supper and bedtime, and so, having cleaned their teeth and put on a warm sweater, the boys went straight to the shelter, remaining there until the all-clear, generally after midnight. Later in the war the shelter was used only when flares were dropped, possibly illuminating the School as a potential target.

As it turned out the School was to escape the war unscathed. The nearest it came to being hit was when two sticks of bombs fell in the village. When

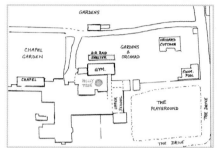

The School in 1940 showing the air raid shelter

a German bomber came down half a mile from the School, the redoubtable Major Bull in his Home Guard uniform from the waist up (but holiday clothes from the waist down) helped to arrest the crew. After the war part of the air raid shelter remained in use as a rifle range well into the 1980s.

Some of the staff were trained as Air Raid Wardens or for the Home Guard, and the boys had their own version of the Home Guard – the TSLI, the Twyford School Light Infantry, which carried out manoeuvres and exercises. Parades were held on the Wednesday half-holiday, and most boys participated; the only exceptions were those who had a carpentry lesson at parade time. Replica pistols and rifles were used – the rifles having been made originally for the Home Guard by a boy's parent – and

A Junkers 88 German bomber crash-landed near Twyford in August 1940

these, together with detailed rules for the game, led to much entertainment for the boys.

Twyford Home Guard
Major J.C. Bull, MC, in charge, is fifth from right, centre row

There was also another topical war game based on naval convoys called 'Blockade Running', which involved the younger and slower boys (the 'merchantmen') running round the School grounds from one base to another, whilst the faster ones (the 'submarines') had to try to catch and thus 'sink' them.

A small, but enduring, change made in 1942, was the formation of houses or School Teams as they were then known. Initially there were only three Teams – Bees, Wasps and Hornets, with the Mosquitoes being formed the following term.

For the latter part of the war the classroom beyond the stage was bolted and barred. This led to much speculation amongst the boys. The Headmaster had been designated the local Food Officer with responsibility for feeding the villagers should there be an invasion. The classroom was filled with sugar and tinned corned beef, although when it was opened after the war it was evident that someone had got in and had taken much of the sugar.

Although the war did not directly affect the boys much, every now and then there was a brutal reminder that the war was real and not a game. Old Twyfordian Tom Lawrie recalled: '*I remember one morning when another boy a little younger than me sobbed continually all through Morning Chapel. It was only*

School Photograph July 1942
Revd and Mrs R.G. Wickham are in the centre of the picture. D.R. (later Lord) Hurd is sitting next to Mrs Wickham, and the future headmaster, D.T. Wickham, is seventh from the right in the front row. Major Bull is on the right hand side of the rear row.

Roll of Honour

Killed on Active Service
We regret to announce the death of Lieut. R.W.V. Hamilton, who was killed while leading a raid on Leros Harbour. He had previously been awarded the DSC for his gallantry during the Fleet Air Arm attack on Taranto.
We regret also to hear that S.F.F. Johnson has been killed in action.

Wounded
Capt. G.R.H. Fielding, RAC

Missing
Second Lieut. H.L. Upcott-Gill, RTC
Pilot Officer J. Still, RAFVR

Prisoners of War
Capt. G.W. Acworth, in Italy
Capt. N.E. Strutt, who has also lost an eye
Lieut. M. Farr

The Twyfordian, July 1941

after the service ended that I learnt that he had been told that morning that his father had been killed on active service in the Royal Air Force.'

The School magazine contained occasional reports from Old Twyfordians who were on active service, and each term it published a Roll of Honour of Twyfordians who were casualties of the war.

An example of one such Roll is shown to the left. The numbers of casualties and awards were not as great as those of the First World War, but the impact of casualties on individual families and the School was just as great. The names of the 49 who died during the war are commemorated in the Memorial Library and the Chapel.

HONOURS AND APPOINTMENTS.

DISTINGUISHED SERVICE ORDER.

Major (temporary Lieut.-Colonel) V. W. Street, O.B.E., M.C., The Rifle Brigade.

Lieut.-Colonel F. P. Barclay, M.C., The Royal Norfolk Regiment.

We have received the following citation of Capt. R. B. T. Morton's Military Cross :—

" The citation states that on the night of February 17th-18th Capt. Morton displayed courage and leadership of the highest order. His Company went into the assault over difficult ground and at once met an intense concentration of fire from enemy machine guns and grenades, at short range. His men were mown down, and within a few minutes complete sections had been wiped out.

" 'Capt. Morton never hesitated. He personally collected his men, led on the remnants of his hard-hit Company and, showing great personal courage and a complete disregard for his own safety, pressed the assault against the enemy, who fiercely contested every yard gained.

" 'A point was reached when this Company, which had started at full war establishment, could muster no more than 23 unwounded men.

" 'By now it was clear that for his Company to advance would mean its ultimate annihilation in what might prove a forlorn hope. Capt. Morton, inspired by a fierce determination to close with and destroy the enemy, organised his few survivors into an assault group, and was preparing to press on in a desperate attempt to reach the battalion objective, which at this time appeared alive with hitherto untouched machine gun nests. At this point, still exposed to a murderous fire, he received orders to dig in.

" 'He rallied his men and organised a defensive position with his slender resources. Ignoring the hostile fire, which by now included shelling and mortaring, Capt. Morton did not rest until his dispositions were completed and all his wounded had been evacuated.' "

The Twyfordian, December 1944

Many Old Twyfordians and friends will wish to offer their deepest sympathy to Major and Mrs. Bull on the loss of their elder son, Martin Bull, who was killed recently fighting in Italy.

The Twyfordian, December 1944

A War Episode

The following is an account of an episode in which an Old Twyfordian, Sub-Lieutenant M.L. Thornewill, played a part.

Late one night recently, six thick-clad and well-armed men were put silently ashore from a schooner on one of the German-held Dodecanese islands.

They were Captain Harden, an Army officer, Sub-Lieutenant M. L. Thornewill, of the Navy, one Army and one Navy telegraphist, and two Greeks.

They scrambled slowly and painfully through darkness, over rocks and thorn-bushes, and spent the night huddled together on a pimple-top of a hill dominating a bay and a town. Their job was to spy out targets for the destroyers Marne and Meteor to bombard later by daylight.

At ten o'clock next morning, Captain Harden and Sub-Lieutenant Thornewill moved from cover and saucily set off across country to get a closer view of an area where they had seen traffic and people moving. It took them an hour to make a journey of only one mile. They were rewarded by the sight of some promising targets in a workshop, working Germans, guns, trenches and barracks.

Wireless sets sent the necessary " tip-off " to Marne and Meteor, lurking handily out to sea, and by mid-afternoon shells from the two ships were crashing home. Four hours later the observation party was back on board the Marne, enjoying a well-earned supper and a drink.

The Twyfordian, March 1945

Some 60 years after his dangerous and stealthy island landings, Mark Thornewill visited the School. After the War he had been ordained as an Anglican priest and had emigrated to the USA where – in 2004 – he was still living. He recounted how, after 'earning' two *tardis* and an *inepti* on the Slate beside the Library door, he was duly given 'six of the best' by Mr McDonell, the Headmaster.

The end of the war came quietly to Twyford. The flag was hoisted, a thanksgiving service was held in the Chapel, and the blackout shutters were put into storage. The boys spent most of the morning holding the Grand Manoeuvres of the TSLI – the Twyford School Light Infantry – as a sort of Victory Parade. After listening to Mr Churchill's speech at three o'clock there was a ceremonial ringing of the School bell for the first time in many a long year by Fred Stratton, the houseman. Bob Wickham, the Headmaster, reported that 'The evening was spent in a Grand Victory Treasure Hunt and, unknown to the boys, the drinking of the one surviving bottle of port which the Headmaster had treasured throughout the war to toast just such an occasion.'

The School had started the war years in a weak position, with a bare economic minimum of about 40 boys, and the School premises heavily mortgaged. The mortgage was a blessing in disguise as it prevented any thought of moving the School elsewhere which might have led to its closure. Although shortages and rationing continued to make some aspects of life difficult, the School soon settled smoothly back into peacetime routine. Familiar faces returned from war service: Charles Mason came back to the Common Room, and Reg Mundy rejoined the garden staff not long before the head gardener, Mr Dick Aslet, retired after serving in that capacity for 32 years.

There was concern about the economy as the war ended and school costs were rising. Nevertheless, in the years after the war preparatory schools enjoyed a long period of prosperity. At Twyford numbers quickly rose to over 60 boys. This was the maximum that could be comfortably accommodated, and for the next few years demand exceeded the places available.

Feeling more confident about the financial health of the School, Mr Wickham turned his attention to the scope of the education that was offered. Academic and pastoral standards compared favourably with other prep schools, but Bob Wickham wished to broaden other aspects of the boys' school life – in improving physical training and what we would today call fitness and healthy living (including teaching the boys 'to abandon youth's prerogative of essential grubbiness'); in learning about the scientific and mechanical things around them; and in training every boy to use, not only his brain, but also his hands (nowadays universal, but quite a new concept at that time for boys destined for the professions). It was not long before the boys were to have an excellent opportunity to practise using these hands.

At times after the Second World War the School hosted the village fête and flower show on the first Saturday in August, which was in those days the Bank Holiday weekend. In this picture, taken c1946, Chris Pearce, the Head Groundsman, is being presented with a trophy by the Headmaster's wife, Betty Wickham, after he and other School employees had won every prize in the adult classes.

Mid Century Miscellany

Bob Wickham relaxing outside the old pavilion c1938. To the left of the picture can be seen the archway through the chalk wall near the modern Sports Hall entrance. The roof of the old 1914 Swimming Bath is also visible.

Prizewinners are listed on the honours boards in the Old Dining Hall. The Vernon Prize for Mathematics was instituted in 1936. F. J. Dyson, the first recipient, became an eminent mathematical physicist, and D.R. Hurd was to become Home Secretary and, later, Foreign Secretary.

For at least 100 years it has been traditional for there to be a large bonfire on Guy Fawkes Night. Long ago it was fashionable to make an effigy of a topical 'baddie' such as the Kaiser, or, on one occasion, a suffragette, (see page 50). There would be four tunnels to the centre of the bonfire into which the four youngest boys would go to light the fire.

Football 1st XI Team

For many years *The Twyfordian* reported without mercy on the performance of the players in the first teams. Woe betide those who could have done better. The right back in the 1950 1st XI football team perhaps wished he had tried harder when he (or his parents) read this report:

> Apparently composed entirely of shins and stomach, off which the ball rebounds whenever he tries to trap it, he has yet contrived to put in some astonishingly effective defence. Adopts an attitude of complete indifference towards the game at odd moments, and seldom kicks any distance in spite of his obvious physical advantages. Has some merit as the team's licensed buffoon.

The Twyfordian, December 1950

The Coronation

> On Friday, June 12th, by invitation of the Admiralty, six boys and the Headmaster were able to go round the Fleet assembled at Spithead for the Coronation Review. Unfortunately the weather was not kind, and rain was heavy at times, and visibility at no time good. Even so, it was a most impressive sight, and a most interesting trip lasting about three hours, in which we covered practically the same course to be taken by the Royal Yacht a few days later. Through the kindness of Mr. Rannie, two other boys were able to go on the Sunday.

The Twyfordian, July 1953

After the war ended, plans were discussed for an appropriate memorial. Accordingly, in 1946 it was decided to place a memorial board in the Chapel and to build a Hobbies and Handicrafts Room from donations made by parents and Old Twyfordians. To minimise the cost of this, the ever-resourceful Bob Wickham decided that the building of the Handicrafts Room should be a School project. The framework of an ex-army hut from Salisbury Plain was requisitioned, and over the next two years the building was erected by staff and boys. It was to serve the School for the next 50 years on a site that is now partly occupied by the new Science School.

Another significant event at this time was the acquisition, in 1948, of the strip of land to the north of the School buildings, between the main road and Mallard's Close *(see page 9)*. This purchase was made possible by the generosity of Mr George Marsh, the former long-serving member of staff.

Freed from the constraints of war, the School flourished in the early 1950s with a wide range of activities. On the stage there were fine performances of ambitious productions including *The Tempest*, *Arsenic and Old Lace*, and Molière's *Le Médecin malgré lui*. In one concert (the future Lord) Moynihan 'acted the part of Moynihan with consummate success, and smoked a cigarette as if to the habit born!'. For one of the productions, *The Children of the Chapel*, the School was lent (and subsequently given) some Stuart panelling which today is on the Old Dining Hall dais. In a single term in 1953 the Chapel Choir sang 26 anthems, which was a considerable feat considering the frequent complexity of such music. A printing press – Twyford Press – was started, on which were printed items such as invitations, play programmes and the term's calendar of events. Hobbies proliferated, among them model railways, model aeroplane making and a stamp club.

In 1947, Bob Wickham, assisted by boys, hand-mixed the concrete and laid the foundations for the War Memorial Hobbies and Handicrafts Room. In the background is Orchard Cottage, the Head Groundsman's house.

The interior of the Hobbies Room is shown here in 1996 towards the end of its life. Woodwork and other practical crafts would in future be taught in the new CDT building. The old Hobbies Room was demolished in 1999 to make way for the new Science School.

G. N. Paterson receiving a shield for the Mosquitoes from Betty Wickham in June 1953
Looking on is the Headmaster, Bob Wickham.

The School was prospering – there were well over 70 boys and the dormitories were crowded. Nevertheless Bob Wickham turned his thoughts to the means by which the School could be placed on a firmer financial foundation. Teachers needed a proper salary structure, but the School could not afford to pay salaries comparable to the state sector. This was hardly surprising as the school fees of £175 per annum had remained unchanged since the end of the First World War whilst overall inflation for that period had been 60%. Aware that there was a wealth of business experience among parents from which the School could benefit, Mr Wickham established a financial Advisory Council comprising some very senior and eminent people from the legal and business worlds. By 1956, Mr Wickham, in a most generous gesture, decided that the future of the School was best assured by the formation of a charitable trust. As a result the Council evolved into Twyford School Trust, the Trust being renamed 'Twyford School' in 2003, which governs the School to this day.

The printing press was started in 1954 and was run by the boys. It produced much of the School's routine stationery, such as calendars, invitations and programmes.

A timeless scene in a 1950s setting. It is Sports Day, and Charles Mason is about to start a race, with Anthony Moynihan close by watching intently. The future Lord Moynihan was to have a colourful life.

By the end of the 1950s it was becoming increasingly clear that public schools were not sufficiently attuned to industrial needs, and this led to greater emphasis being placed on Science and Technology. Bob Wickham, through his membership, and chairmanship in 1963 and 1964, of the Incorporated Association of Preparatory Schools (IAPS), became a leading advocate of the introduction of Science into prep schools, and his own School was to be an early beneficiary.

1959 was a Jubilee year for the School, as it celebrated 150 years on its present site. A dinner was held in the Easter holidays at the Café Royal in London at which the guest of honour was the former Headmaster, Mr H.C. McDonell. The dinner was attended by 280 Old Twyfordians (the oldest of whom had left Twyford in 1894) together with other members of the Twyford community. One of the speakers, a Governor, Admiral Sir William Andrewes, said he vividly recalled the excellence of the Centenary lunch half a century previously. In the Summer term, the boys had their own celebration outing to the Royal Tournament in London, travelling in King Alfred Motor Services buses, and stopping for picnics during the journey.

Four years later, in 1963, Bob Wickham retired as Headmaster after 26 years of outstanding and selfless service to the

School, and was succeeded by his son, David Wickham, who was supported by his wife, Jenny. David had been educated at Twyford and Winchester, and had then read Mathematics and Science at Oxford. He had been a teacher at Tonbridge, and Jenny too had been a teacher. After relinquishing the headship, Bob Wickham was to remain as Chaplain and teacher at the School for many years thereafter, and indeed was still teaching woodwork over 20 years later.

The School had started the 1960s in good shape. There were about 86 boys – the maximum the School could take – the waiting lists were full until 1971, and the School's financial position was sound. However, change was afoot in the prep school world. By the mid 1960s a number of new educational developments were bringing change: the spoken word became an integral

(*top*) Long Room dormitory in about 1983. The bed with the red cover is that of the Dormitory Senior.

(*middle*) The first language laboratory was built in 1970 as part of a group of rooms also providing space for science, carpentry, and music practice. It was on the site of what is now the workshop area of the Craft, Design and Technology (CDT) building.

(*bottom*) This 1983 picture depicts a well-known, if not necessarily well-loved, scene for generations of boys. The boys' bathroom was built in 1970 and remained unchanged for 30 years, when, in a modest nod to the changing world, some baths were replaced by curtained showers. It was not until 2008 that the last of the small baths were replaced by showers.

part of learning French, and radio and television became essential educational tools. At Twyford there was a growing interest in things outside the School: a party of boys visited a climbing school in Kent, and groups joined the 'Schools Ship' – initially MS Dunera, and later SS Nevasa and SS Uganda – which cruised around the Mediterranean each Easter holidays. About this time a Pioneer Club was founded, which soon evolved into a camping club run by Noel Keble Williams. The boys would set up camp at weekends on sites offered by parents. This started the enduring and popular tradition of the leavers' camp, which for many years has been held in France towards the end of the children's final term.

The next phase of building development was funded by an appeal held in 1968 which raised £56,000. It included the construction in 1970 of a new science laboratory, carpenters' workshop, language laboratory and several music practice rooms. Although none of those buildings exists today – the present Craft, Design and Technology (CDT) building occupies their site – they were nevertheless important and innovative improvements for the School. At the same time, a new bathroom and changing room block was built on the site of the previous one, incorporating on its first floor, accommodation for matrons, a surgery and a large boarders' bathroom. This block remains in use, although in 2008 the last of the boys' baths were replaced by showers. Outside, two hard tennis courts were built to the west of Mallard's Close, and the exit drive from the School was routed into Bourne Lane which made a one-way system possible, resulting in much improved safety for vehicles entering and leaving the School grounds.

© www.fotoflite.com

SS UGANDA CRUISE 1977

'Life in the ship – what is it really like?.... If at sea, the time is divided between deck games, swimming, lectures on places to be visited or the running of the ship, classroom periods when letters are written, logs written up and a number of other activities. In the evenings there were films, quizzes, a fun fair, frog-racing, a fancy dress competition and the inevitable nightly disco. All one can say is that there are few dull moments, and these are generally filled by views of places one passed, Odysseus' Ithaca, Navarino Bay, Cape Matapan, the Dardanelles, the monasteries of Mount Athos, Scylla and Charybdis, even of Stromboli rather half-heartedly doing its stuff and an occasional flock of playful dolphins, all to the accompaniment of helpful comment over the loud-speakers from the bridge.'

The Twyfordian, April 1977

In 1965, Mr McDonell, the former Headmaster, died at the age of 82. Then in 1972, one of the legends of Twyford School also died: Major Bull had joined the staff in 1905 and thereafter devoted 56 years of his life to teaching mathematics to generations of Twyfordians and their sons. He helped, in no small measure, to shape the School that we know today. Amongst those he taught was the young Freeman Dyson, now a famous theoretical physicist and mathematician. Even at the age of 90, Major Bull was still a regular supporter at School matches.

A small school is particularly vulnerable to general economic conditions and the 1970s was a period of financial insecurity: in 1975 inflation reached 24%. Before the Second World War a school of 30 to 60 pupils was financially viable, but by the 1970s a prep school needed 100 to 160 pupils to be secure. In the seven years from 1970 forty prep schools closed, and almost all the schools which closed after 1973 had fewer than 70 pupils. Despite the country's economic situation Twyford maintained an average of 89 boys during the 1970s, reaching a maximum of 95 in 1979. Nevertheless, throughout this decade Governors and Trustees, in common with those of many other schools, gave recurrent consideration to the size of the School roll, and the possible introduction of girls and day children. This would produce educational as well as financial benefits. These deliberations were to lead, in the 1980s, to a major expansion of the School and in 1977 there were early harbingers of the changes ahead. The School started accepting day boys, and the Headmaster's elder two daughters, Vanessa and Diana, were admitted as special cases. They were joined later by their siblings Robert and Sarah. The only girl known to have attended the School before this was Kathleen White, the daughter of Major General White who lived in Mallard's Close early in the twentieth century.

Gardens and Grounds Staff
The team in the late 19th century (*above*), and (*below*), 100 years later, their successors Bob Unsworth, Ted Unsworth, and Michael Dean, photographed in 1983. The people have changed but the besom broom looks remarkably similar.

The School Farm

As well as having vegetable gardens, the School had a small dairy farm in the fields either side of Bourne Lane. The farm buildings were on Bourne Lane in the corner of Home Close field, just to the south east of the present School grounds – where Bourne Lodge now stands.

Fred Oxford was the cowman for many years, as was his nephew Tom, and at the time of writing, fourth and fifth generation members of the same family are part of the catering staff. The earliest mention of the farm is a recollection by Bob Wickham of a visit that he made as a small boy shortly before 1910:

'The firmest memory is of Mr Oxford and his cows, and particularly of my surprised discovery that every cow had its name and its stall, and that they would all come when called. I remember the large shallow pans from which one could skim off the cream. I can still picture Tom striding up to the School, two large milk pails hanging from the yoke across his shoulders. I cannot remember seeing the cream being churned into butter, though this was certainly not abandoned until some time after this visit, the churns being geared to a shaft driven by the pony as he ceaselessly – or nearly ceaselessly – circled the pony well and pumped the School water supply at the same time.'

Tom Oxford died in 1957, but Major Bull continued managing the farm as he had done since 1938. The farm was still of considerable value to the School, not only for milk, but for hay. In 1964, *The Twyfordian* reported: *'We had a wonderful hay crop, picking up over two thousand bales from seventeen acres. We sold seven hundred bales.'*

By this time Major Bull was in his 84th year, and another member of the teaching staff, Noel Keble Williams, took over the running of the farm. During the next three years he both doubled the herd to 28 Guernsey milking cows and increased the yield of milk per cow substantially. In 1967 the herd produced 17,798 gallons, and this provided a substantial contribution to the School's income.

This proved to be the farm's high noon. By 1971 it was struggling. Expensive new pasteurisation equipment had to be installed, and there were ongoing problems with operating it. The small herd was barely viable. The farm had quickly become a relic of a bygone age and in 1978 it was closed.

Tom Oxford

An ambitious plan had been drawn up in 1978 for a new development to include improved sports facilities, classrooms and a modern dining hall, less exposed than the old one to the increasing volume and size of passing, pre-M3, traffic. An appeal raised a noteworthy £95,000 but, in the event, owing to the economic situation and high inflation, it was only possible to build the present dining hall, which was opened in 1981 and named the Wickham Hall. Nevertheless, this was the start of the major changes of the next two decades, and the School life depicted in these photographs was soon to belong to the past.

These scenes, although taken at the end of David Wickham's headship, will be familiar to many generations of Twyfordians.

Upper School in the 1970s
The picture shows 'Readings' after lunch, as seen from the stage. It was the fashion in those days that 'digestion should be given opportunity before exercise'. Mr Payne, the History master, is supervising the boys from the 'Throne'.

The Dining Hall in the 1970s
Laid for lunch. The floors are gleaming, every knife and fork is carefully placed, and familiar portraits line the walls.

The Throne
The Headmaster's 'Throne' (*left*) was probably acquired by the Revd J.C. Bedford when he built Upper School in 1819.

Now the old order was changing. Charles Mason's 50 years on the staff were celebrated at a special summer gathering in 1982, and he was to retire two years later. The following year the long stewardship of the School by the Wickham family drew to a close upon the retirement of David Wickham, and his wife Jenny, in 1983. David had nurtured the School successfully during two decades of educational change and, latterly, financial stringency. He handed over to his successor a school with a firm foundation upon which to build its future. His departure marked the end of a total of 110 years of Wickham family headship and well over 150 years as members of the staff. The Chairman of Governors wrote in his annual report: 'To the end they have put the School first and themselves second.' That was written of David and Jenny Wickham, but equally could be said of generations of the Wickham family who served the School so selflessly.

David Wickham subsequently was a member of the Trust for a period early in the new millennium, and remains an unrivalled fount of knowledge concerning the history of the School.

David Wickham's Retirement
David (*above*) with a group of senior boys towards the end of his final term in the summer of 1983 and (*right*) with his wife, Jenny.

Charles Mason Day 1982
A marquee has stood on its present site near both house and kitchens for 130 years. Framed by the mulberry tree, parents and staff on 'Charles Mason Day' enjoy tea outside the marquee, a scene familiar to all for decades.

In his farewell speech David Wickham said, 'There comes a time when a gentle shake is needed to stir the dust, break the cobwebs and shed light into dark corners.' The person that the Governors appointed to succeed David Wickham in 1983 certainly did that. Richard Gould was an adventurous choice and a colourful character. He came from the Royal Hong Kong Jockey Club where he was a stipendiary steward. He was a shrewd judge of character and, with his business acumen, it was not long before change was afoot. Both he and his wife, Jane, had previous prep school experience – Richard as a schoolmaster at Summer Fields, Oxford, and Jane as a matron and a headmaster's secretary. It was their experience, coupled with his energy and vision, that was to transform Twyford.

When the Goulds arrived there were 96 pupils in the School. In recent years, as previously mentioned, it had become apparent that Twyford would have to increase its size if it were to remain financially viable, and prep school parents in general were now expecting a cosier and less austere environment than had been traditionally provided in schools such as Twyford. Demand was rising for day places and for co-education and, increasingly, children came from families which lived locally.

Initially some low-cost small changes were made. Key areas of the School – such as the 'backcourts' – were painted by the new Headmaster himself! The dormitories were carpeted (these carpets proved to be long-lasting and were still in place 23 years later), central heating was installed in the three unheated dormitories and Upper School was carpeted and curtained. The first three computers for educational use were donated and this heralded a new era. More significantly, however, it was decided to open a Pre-Prep department. Serle's Hill was accordingly converted to become the Pre-Prep which opened with two classes of boys and girls and two

teachers in September 1985. The girls in these classes were the first to enter the School on a regular basis.

The opening of the Pre-Prep marked a moment of fundamental change: from being a school for boys aged 8 – 13, Twyford progressively became a co-educational school for children aged 3 – 13. The Pre-Prep provided the 'seedcorn' for entry into the Prep School, and this enhanced financial stability. Stablecross – later the Pre-Prep nursery – was built as accommodation for staff who had vacated Serle's Hill. Stablecross is named after the School stables that had been sited nearby and the 'cross' which forms an architectural detail on the gable end.

Richard and Jane Gould
with their daughters, Annie and Zosie

Old School Room Dormitory 1983
The iron bedsteads were later replaced by single beds with wooden headboards, and the floors were fully carpeted.

The Computer Club in the Library, Spring 1983
'At last the new Computer has arrived! The BBC Acorn has a colour monitor and a multiplicity of functions, and now "graphics" is our new treasure. Well, not quite! The actual computer arrived with a tape deck that did not work and without a colour monitor. Never mind! We have managed for two years with "Black and White": a little longer won't hurt.'   *The Twyfordian, April 1983*

Picking Raspberries in the Walled Garden 1983

A Woodwork Class c1983

Farm Visit 1984

A party of boys visiting Mr and Mrs J. Fairey's Manor Farm at Houghton in July 1984. Noel Keble Williams, wearing a tie, is seated next to his wife, Joyce.

Soon change was taking place across all areas of the School. Plans were being made for new buildings, catering was contracted out, and the School was being marketed. A new School name logo was adopted, and a cartoon picture of a tortoise and hare  under a banner proclaiming the School motto '*Vince Patientia*' ('It's dogged as does it') made its first appearance. New staff were appointed and a tutor system was introduced. Much good work was being done in the classroom by staff and pupils alike and, gratifyingly for everyone, five scholarships and awards were won by boys in 1988.

So far as the children were concerned, there were numerous extra-curricular activities and clubs to supplement the academic fare: judo, golf, photography, cooking, astronomy, model making, drama, shooting and chess. Noel Keble Williams had opened a School shop, which Richard Gould called 'Taffy's' – an allusion to N.K.W.'s Welsh origins.

Family social occasions became a feature of School life when the Twyford Parents' Association (TPA) was formed in 1984. The first event was a very successful barbecue and barn dance. Over the next 25 years the TPA was to organise numerous popular entertainments.

Reflecting changes in education generally, a Craft, Design and Technology department was formed, allowing children a greater opportunity to develop various practical skills. Art facilities were also improved. Various sports were encouraged and the Headmaster reported that on any one winter's afternoon there might be rugby, squash, swimming, tennis, shinty, cross-country running and judo taking place.

Summer Scenes 1988

Prize-giving
Sports Day has always been one of the highlights of the year. Prize-giving on the lawn was followed by tea in the marquee.

Putting Green

This was adjacent to the newly-built Garden Cottage which is at the top left of the picture. The new Classroom 2 can be seen in the top right corner.

Sports Day Tug of War

In 1985 the School roll exceeded 100 for the first time, and by 1987 this had increased to 148 with a further 62 children in the new Pre-Prep. The waiting lists were full to 1992 and, buoyed by optimism for the future, the Governors approved a programme for a major development of classrooms and other important facilities.

This was not easy as the School lay in a conservation area. However, with the help of an eminent planning consultant, Elizabeth (later Dame Elizabeth) Chesterton, approval was gained for a far-reaching development plan. It then fell to the newly appointed Bursar, John Stott, to manage a seemingly endless stream of exciting projects. This he did with the imaginative help of landscape and planning specialists, Rik and Ayda Sturdy, architect Peter Parkman (of Galloway and Partners), and the local building contractors, Don and Steven Short. It was not until 15 years later that the work was completed.

The sale of Mallard's Close financed the building, in 1987, of eight new classrooms and two science laboratories. A few months later a major appeal for the new Sports Hall was launched at a dinner held on Saturday, 17 October 1987. This was an inauspicious date as it turned out: the dinner was sandwiched between the 'great gale' the previous day, and the stock market crash on Black Monday two days later. Nevertheless, the funds were quickly raised and the second phase of the development started.

Orchard Cottage, the old wooden bungalow, had been occupied over the years by various staff ranging from butler to groundsman, but it had to be demolished to make room for the new Sports Hall. This ambitious hall, incorporating an enlarged swimming pool on the site of the old one, was completed in September 1989, and a time capsule was buried outside the entrance. The Sports Hall was formally opened three months later by the Rt Hon Douglas Hurd CBE, MP, the Foreign Secretary and one of Twyford's most eminent Old Boys.

(*above*) Douglas Hurd in the Library talking to boys during his visit to open the Sports Hall in December 1989.

(*left*) Burying the time capsule. Holding the spades are the Headmaster, Richard Gould (left), and Don Short whose construction company was responsible for the building work involved. The capsule contained various artefacts including a music cassette, School photographs and a camera.

1914-1988

1980s

THE
SWIMMING POOL

Prior to 1914, when the first Swimming Bath was built, the boys swam at a bathing place in the nearby River Itchen. The original Swimming Bath (*left, upper and lower*) was an innovation ahead of its time. To heat the water, steam from the adjacent boiler was injected under pressure into the bath. In later years Archie, the elderly gardener, would coax the ancient boiler with best Welsh steam coal in an attempt to raise steam. The bath lasted for 75 years and looked much the same throughout its life.
The new pool (*right, upper and lower*) was built on the site of the old bath in 1989. The original Swimming Bath was 12.3m by 6m; this pool measures 20m by 6.6m, and has a maximum depth in the centre of 1.8m.

1989

2006

With increasing numbers there was a need for additional playing fields. Hitherto the grounds in front of the main School were picturesque but small. The old, smaller cricket field was located on the western half of today's cricket ground. The pavilion stood beside the yew tree, and the practice nets were several feet below the site of the modern 1st XI cricket square. In a major development of the grounds, the present car park was built on what had been the Playground since at least the mid nineteenth century. The original cricket ground was extended to the east, and the levelling of this whole area produced not only a mountain of Hampshire chalk, but also the fine cricket ground that we know today. The first matches were played on the new ground in 1991.

Apart from these extensive external developments, the building of the new classrooms enabled many improvements to be made inside the School. Some former classrooms became recreational day rooms; the seating capacity of Upper School was increased by adding a balcony; the Old Dining Hall was renovated; the Library was improved; and a classroom was equipped with 16 BBC Acorn computers.

The Playground (*left*)
This 1985 view looking westward towards the School house shows the original Playground as it was for much of the School's existence. It became the main car park in 1989 when the playing fields were redeveloped. It is the same view as the 1848 painting on page 7.

The Cricket Ground
For most of the 20th century the cricket ground was to the south of the ha-ha (*right*). Major earthworks were required to make the fine cricket ground shown in this 2007 photograph (*below*).

Twyford in Transition 1988

This photograph shows the School in a state of transition. The first eight new classrooms and two laboratories have been built. The old Playground bordered by the School drive remains, as do the old cricket ground and pavilion. The former Swimming Bath and Orchard Cottage are still to be seen, and Garden Cottage is under construction. The tractor shed is on the corner where the Music School now stands. The Headmaster's House has not yet been built, and the Goulds live on the first floor of the School's main house.

The Pre-Prep Department

The Pre-Prep occupies Serle's Hill, a late Victorian house in the School grounds. Its location was ideal for the purpose – the Pre-Prep would be far enough from the Prep School to allow it some autonomy, and yet near enough to enjoy its facilities. It opened in September 1985 with two classes and a total of 21 boys and girls. The first significant addition to the buildings was a new assembly hall, added in 1994, which nestles comfortably in a corner of an old walled garden.

The Pre-Prep grew steadily, and by the year 2000 there were six classes totalling 100 children. The nearby Stablecross bungalow became the Nursery in the same year. This allowed space for various improvements including provision of a children's computer room in the main Pre-Prep building. The next major change was to occur in 2008 when the top year group – Year 3 – became part of the Prep School.

Mrs Susan Ouvry was the Head of the Pre-Prep Department for its formative six years and was succeded by Mrs Sally Thompson who had been a founding member of the staff. Mrs Thompson was Head from 1991-2007, very successfully guiding its continued expansion and development, creating a happy and stable environment for young children at the start of their school lives.

Over the years the curriculum has always been wide-ranging, and none more so than nowadays. In addition to the main academic subjects, outings, art and craft, music and drama, and sporting activities are just as much evident in the Pre-Prep as they are in the Prep School.

Mrs Karen Rogers took over as Head of the Pre-Prep Department in 2007 on the retirement of Mrs Thompson.

Serle's Hill 2009
Serle's Hill house was built as a sanatorium in 1896-1897 during the diphtheria epidemics. It was, however, never used as a sick house as it was too large and too far from the main School buildings for its original purpose. Instead it was used mainly as staff accommodation until 1985 when the house became the home of the new Pre-Prep Department.

The Pre-Prep 1998

Pre-Prep Year 1 – 1998
Mrs Sally Thompson (*rear row, right*) is Head of the Pre-Prep Department and Class Teacher.
Mrs Wendy Criddle (*left*) is the Class Assistant.

Anne Anscombe
(now Hibberd), a
Pre-Prep Year 2
teacher since 1986.

Karen Rogers,
Head of the
Pre-Prep
Department
from 2007.

Stablecross – The Nursery 2009

A Lunchtime Crocodile 2009
A familiar sight – Pre-Prep children wend their way to lunch
accompanied by Sarah Rolfe (née Waters).

101 ✦

As the new decade of the 1990s opened it was clear that the School had been transformed successfully into a thriving modern prep school able to compete with the demands of the contemporary market. By 1987 the School had doubled in size, and in 1992 there were 181 children in the Prep School together with 75 in the Pre-Prep. There had been 18 academic and administrative staff in 1983: now there were 42. The range of activities was wider than ever and, after a break of four years during which all attention had been concentrated on expansion, *The Twyfordian* resumed publication.

Oliver 1993

A glance at copies of *The Twyfordian* of that time reveals a wealth of activity and achievement. As well as academic success, there were five music ensembles including an orchestra and a jazz band – despite the very modest music facilities; and performances of ambitious shows including *The Mikado*, *Oliver,* and *Calamity Jane.* There was also success in other areas such as technology competitions and, in particular, history: each year the School did

very well in the Townsend Warner History competition under the guidance of Anthony Lafferty, Head of History, and in 1994 the team won first prize, beating 100 other schools.

Sports teams blossomed, with many boys playing for the School – from 1st XI cricket to shinty (which enabled those with more modest sporting prowess to enjoy away matches and match teas). In these years the School teams enjoyed outstanding success: the Colts football XI of 1991 won all 15 games played, and two years later the 1st XI and Colts cricket teams lost only one match between them, with six boys representing Hampshire. The tennis teams

Calamity Jane 1994

won all their matches. In 1994 the 1st XI cricket team had a most successful tour to Barbados, playing against all the top Barbadian school teams, and winning six out of seven matches.

Despite recession and economic gloom, there was sufficient confidence and funding for the next phase of the development programme to proceed. In 1993 two additional classrooms (the present classrooms 11 and 12) and the Music School were built.

Hitherto, there had been one dedicated music classroom with a piano, and four small practice rooms. Now, the new Music School contained a large performance room and many practice rooms, together with a small open-air theatre built on classical lines with curved stone seating – an ideal setting for occasional summer lunchtime recitals.

Hockey 1990s

Barbados Cricket Tour 1994

Prizes
Headmaster, Richard Gould, and Second Master, Greg Bishop, preparing for prize-giving in the summer of 1995.

The Music School mid 1990s

The Dining Hall in the 1980s
This scene will be very familiar to many Old Twyfordians. Nowadays Dean Wilkins, the Catering Manager, and his team serve lunch to 450 children and staff in an hour and a half.

Boys' Toys c1990
These desks or 'toys' were in the classroom to the left of the locker corridor near Upper School. They were used by senior boys for prep and had been made by Rob Forder (*inset*) who was the School Caretaker in the 1980s and 1990s.

The Computer Room c1991
This room was opposite the Geography classroom and is now part of the main corridor. The computers are BBC Archimedes.

Taffy's

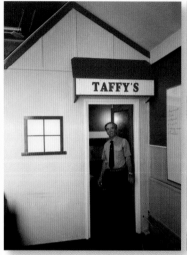

Over the years, the peripatetic School shop has occupied many sites, from cupboards to kitchen cabinets. Its finest hour came during the 1990s when it had its own premises in a corner of the classroom adjacent to the Upper School stage.

Long-serving members of the School community, Noel and Joyce Keble Williams, formally retired in 1993, although Noel was to remain for a further five years assisting the support staff. On his final retirement he presented a hornbeam tree which was planted on the southern boundary of the cricket pitch. Dedicated and energetic, Noel had been the lynchpin of the School staff since 1959, and had turned his hand to many tasks. Nominally Head of Geography, it was Noel who took parties of children to cruises on the 'Schools Ship'; established the Pioneer (camping) Club; ran the School shop, and various sports teams (particularly shinty). He also managed the School dairy farm for many years. Generations of boys learnt their geography from a map of the world on the ceiling of his classroom – it is still there to this day – and parents will remember his warm welcome when they visited the School, and his remarkable memory for names.

1993 was marked by the death at the age of 87 of the former Headmaster, Revd R.G. Wickham, known to all as Bob. It was Bob who saved the School from almost certain closure when he took over as Headmaster in 1937. Brian Trubshaw, of Concorde fame, who arrived as a young boy in a school almost without electricity, had two terms with the new Headmaster and described the changes he made as 'fantastic'. Douglas Hurd, the former Foreign Secretary, who joined the School early in Bob's time, had the warmest recollections of his youthful humanity, and of the kindness of his wife Betty, and said that Bob taught him to want to be a scholar.

As well as serving as Headmaster for very many years, Bob had been School Chaplain for even longer. After relinquishing the headship, he remained the Chaplain for a further 21 years until 1984. Long after he died, during a periodic spring clean of the vestry, a large collection of termly pupil lists was discovered. On the reverse sides of these sheets Bob had written his sermon notes, covering the entire period of his headship. Fortunately these survived by chance, and provide a fascinating record of how he tried to impart principles of the Christian faith to generations of boys – suggesting in Chapel, for instance, that Remembrance Sunday for them was 'remembering two wars that you don't remember'.

It was decided that the most fitting memorial to Bob Wickham would be a renovation of the Chapel, which had been built by his grandfather. The restoration was completed in 1996, one hundred and one years after his uncle, Charles Wickham, had improved and extended the Chapel. Bob Wickham was described in a fitting phrase as an 'innovating traditionalist' and was one of the most influential figures of the preparatory school world in the post-war years.

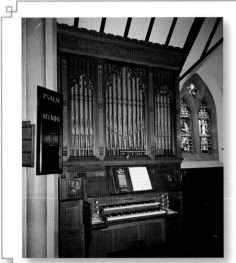

The Chapel

This is one of the hidden treasures of Victorian Hampshire.

The Chapel Organ

The fine small organ, built by J.W. Walker & Sons, was installed in 1870 in the south eastern corner of the Chapel. It was a gift from Mr J.C. Heriz Smith, former Second Master who was a member of staff from 1866-1870. The organ is thought to have been brought from its previous location, a house in South London, by train from Nine Elms. Prior to the installation of electricity, the organ was hand-pumped by a boy. The instrument was enlarged in 1895 by the addition of a swell organ and was moved to its present position. In 1924 a new organ case in oak was fitted – this was a gift from the Revd C.T. Wickham. The organ underwent a major restoration in 2005.

In 1994 the next stage of development took place with the construction, as previously mentioned, of the Pre-Prep assembly hall, and girls' boarding accommodation. This was followed in 1997 by the Craft, Design and Technology building, named after Mr Gould. The upper floor contains a computer suite and an art room where colourful displays catch the visitor's eye.

The CDT Building

Downstairs, in the fine technology workshop, children design and build everything from puzzles and games to pieces of furniture.

A name familiar to many generations of Old Twyfordians finally slipped from the formal roll in the middle of the decade. Charles Mason's links with the School were first forged in 1932 when he joined the staff from Oxford, a year before David Wickham was born. He served at the School throughout the latter's headship, retiring in 1984. Thereafter he regularly attended School matches, and served as a Trustee until 1995, a year before his death at the age of 87. Charles Mason was a traditional 'schoolmaster' who devoted his working life to the School. He was one of those who made Twyford what it is today, and his name lives on in the School: 'Mason' is now the formal name for the 'Mosquitoes' House, and there is a commemorative bench in the grounds.

Charles Mason

Mr Mark Lowth stood down as Chairman of the Trust in 1996. He had been guiding and supporting the School as a Governor and Trustee for 31 years. Five generations of his family had been at the School since 1815 – a noteworthy record in Twyford's history. A copy of a letter written by Charles Lowth, one of the first generation of the Lowth family to attend the School, can be seen on page 14.

Richard Gould
In a field of his own
on Sports Day in June 1995.

Richard Gould, having expended so much time and energy in reshaping and developing Twyford over 13 years, decided to embark on a new career at the end of 1996. Supported by the Governors of the day, he had wrought a remarkable regeneration and transformation in the fortunes of the School. On his arrival in 1983, he had focused immediately on substantially increasing the School roll, at the same time shaping Twyford for the future.

Susie Mason, was the Matron from 1994 to 2010. Many Twyfordians will remember her kindness and dedication. In this picture she is reading a bedtime story to some of the younger boarders.

The Headmaster, Richard Gould, at an end of term gathering in the west courtyard in July 1994.

The appointment of new staff, the switch to co-education, the opening of the Pre-Prep, the introduction of flexi-boarding and a wide-ranging, ambitious development plan were just some of the ways by which Richard Gould achieved this. During his time, the School roll increased dramatically from about 96 to 270, the maximum agreed by the Governors at that time.

The immense, but sympathetic, changes to the physical character of the School should not obscure what Richard and Jane Gould considered their most important role: they were dedicated to the well-being and happiness of all the children in their care.

Understanding, encouragement and consideration for others were the key words in the Twyford ethos. With the enthusiastic support of the staff, they worked tirelessly in creating and maintaining a happy and positive environment, where all could thrive. Parents and Twyfordians of the day will testify to their success.

Nigel Goodall, Head of CDT, helping children in the new CDT workshop.

Rosy Greenleaf (*above*), Head of Art, taking a class in the new Art Room.

Several totem poles made by children in the pottery workshop are on permanent display in the School.

Familiar Faces

(*left*) **Rose Job** was the School Secretary between 1980 and 1995.

(*centre*) **Penny Unwin** has been Headmaster's Secretary since 1997.

(*right*) Four Royal Navy Bursars: (*left to right*) **John Stott** (1982-1998); **Roger Porteous** (1998-2006); **Rob Bosshardt** (2006-2009); **John Murphie** (from 2009).

(*left*) **'The Workforce'** who maintain the buildings and grounds, in 2003.

(*centre*) **Dorothy (Dot) James** was a familiar figure at innumerable match teas and other catering events for 37 years. She was the third of five generations of the Oxford family who have served the School. Today her daughter and granddaughters help with the catering.

(*right*) **Chris Farmer**, **Pam Andrews**, and **Sue Lockwood**, the three sisters, are well-known faces at Twyford, having been at the School since the 1980s. They have served countless lunches to pupils and staff and in this June 1999 picture are enjoying their own lunch under the mulberry tree near the marquee.

(*left*) **Margaret Gardner**, joined in 1975, and retired as Day Matron in 2009.

(*centre*) **Moira and Tony Goodburn** who served the School from 1986-2009, Tony as Head of French and, later, Librarian, and Moira as a member of the administrative staff.

(*right*) **Tony Francis** (*left*), Old Twyfordian, and Head of Science, pictured in 2009, with his former Geography teacher **Noel Keble Williams** who, 46 years previously, had written some less than complimentary reports on Tony. One of them states: '*A very poor term. There has been no showing of effort or concentration and very little progress made.*'

Mr Philip Fawkes became Headmaster in 1996. He came from Lathallan School in Scotland, where he had been Headmaster. At Twyford, he took over a thriving school, but which, like many others, had declining full boarding numbers. Many of the children lived locally, whereas in earlier days, few had done so; now their parents wanted them at home for the weekends. Partly as a consequence, flexi-boarding, whereby children spent one or more nights a week boarding, was becoming increasingly popular and Philip Fawkes continued to encourage this with much success. This, coupled with weekly boarding, enabled Twyford to retain its boarding ethos even though the majority of children were day children. The proportion of girls rose as parents recognised that Twyford was a family school which encouraged siblings of either gender.

Philip Fawkes with Children c1997

Under the aegis of Philip Fawkes, a new Science School was built in 1999 and was opened by Professor Richard Dawkins, Professor of the Public Understanding of Science, Oxford. To build the Science School, the old Hobbies Room, built by Bob Wickham and the boys of the School as a Second World War memorial, unfortunately had to be demolished. An oak commemorative plaque now marks the site of the War Memorial Hobbies and Handicrafts Room.

Upstairs Girls' Dormitory

(*above*) The formal opening of the Science School in March 2000 by Professor Richard Dawkins. Mr Fawkes, Headmaster, and Mr J.A.W. Francis, Head of Science, are standing near the entrance.

(*below*) One of the two new Science Laboratories.

Philip Fawkes departed in 2002. The School had grown and prospered during his tenure. There had been changes in the structuring of classes and the pupil roll increased to the then highest figure ever – 312 children. The School was full and had healthy waiting lists, and excellent academic results had been achieved. There were by this time two very well equipped Information Technology teaching suites and the whole School – classrooms and administrative offices - had been fitted with a networked IT system.

Greg Bishop
Second Master

Greg Bishop, the Second Master, who had joined the School as Head of Maths in 1989, became Acting Headmaster for three terms. The School continued to run smoothly under his calm leadership prior to the arrival of Dr David Livingstone, the new Headmaster, in 2003.

Dr Livingstone came from Rugby where he had been Head of Geography, a Housemaster, and a Deputy Head. As a keen hockey player he was pleased to see that the next major development planned was the construction of an all weather pitch. This was built on what former generations of Twyfordians knew as the Barley Field. Whilst its appearance is scarcely one to warm a poet's heart compared with the broad sweep of the greensward of the old Barley Field, the all weather pitch has proved to be a most valuable facility for the School. It was formally opened in February 2007 by an Old Twyfordian, Rob Moore, a hockey player at international level, who had been a member of some of the School's

David Livingstone
Headmaster

All Weather Pitch 2009

very successful sports teams of the early 1990s. Another significant addition to the playing fields was the leasing of part of Home Close field to the south of the School grounds.

Finally, in 2008, a number of projects that had long been in gestation came to fruition in a period of frenetic activity. The girls' boarding accommodation in the Chapel garden was converted into two maths classrooms, whilst the dormitories were refurbished and the girls moved upstairs. The Central Hall and its main staircase were restored to their former glory by the removal of the fire screens which had been in place since the mid-1970s. This was made possible with modern technology.

The transfer of Year 3, from the Pre-Prep to the main School, necessitated additional classrooms. Consequently, a new classroom

Central Hall 2008

and changing room complex, named Saxon Court, was built to the north of the existing classrooms. It incorporated the only remaining walnut tree in the School grounds.

Professor Freeman Dyson at the opening of Saxon Court

A Saxon Grave

Walnut Tree and Saxon Court

Saxon Court was formally opened in February 2009 by Professor Freeman Dyson, an Old Twyfordian and one of the world's most eminent mathematical physicists. He was on this occasion wearing a tie bearing the formula 'E=mc²' which had been given to him by Albert Einstein.

In excavating the foundations of this new development, a Saxon burial ground with 18 graves had been uncovered. These included small children, adult males with the remains of their weaponry, and women with glass bead jewellery thought to have been made from salvaged Roman glass. All, it is believed, were buried in the 8th century. They had lain undiscovered for over 1,200 years. In comparison with this, the 200-year existence of Twyford School on the site seems a mere trifle.

Children of the New Century
Alice in Wonderland 2003
Netball 2005
Team Colours 2007
Music Scholars 2007
Pre-Prep 2008

Although the School itself is well over 200 years old, it moved to its present site in 1809. It is the occupation of the house which has symbolised it for so long, that was commemorated in 1909 and, again, in 2009.

In 1909 the centenary celebrations took place on one memorable summer's day. The celebrations in 2009, in contrast, were marked by a series of varied events, both large and small, spread throughout the year. These involved governors, staff, Old Twyfordians, parents and, most importantly, children. To start the year a special School Tea-Party was held at which the School's newly-designed Coat of Arms was presented by the Lancaster Herald from the College of Arms. Winchester Cathedral provided a fine setting for a Service of Thanksgiving in March. A memorable Old Twyfordian Day in May coincided with the opening of a stunning Exhibition of Art and Design featuring work by current pupils and eminent Old Twyfordians.

On 6 June, at a Super Extravaganza for children and their parents, the Band of the Adjutant General's Corps of the British Army played, in full dress uniform – just as, on 24 June 1909, the Band of the Hampshire Regiment had entertained the guests of the

Super Extravaganza
Children and parents marching behind the Band of the Adjutant General's Corps

day. A Summer Ball and a light-hearted Sports Dinner hosted by David Gower, a Twyford parent and former England Cricket Captain, each provided entertainment for parents and friends. Finally, during the year there were some fascinating talks by experts, covering subjects as diverse as Lewis Carroll's close relationship with the School, Twyford's literary connections, and the story of Concorde – on this occasion by Christopher Orlebar, an Old Twyfordian pilot of the supersonic aircraft.

Presentation of Coat of Arms
Mr Sean Kelly, Chairman of Governors
(*left*) with the Lancaster Herald

During the course of the year, David Livingstone left Twyford having overseen the completion of various projects. By September, the pupil roll had increased to 376 children – the highest it had ever been. Mr Nick Brodrick took over as interim Headmaster for the Autumn term and kept a reassuring hand on the tiller pending the arrival of the new Headmaster. The carol service in Winchester Cathedral was a fitting end to a memorable year.

Twyford School

Thanksgiving Service

on the occasion of the

200th Anniversary
of moving to School House

Friday 20th March 2009 at 11.00am

Winchester Cathedral

Old Twyfordian Day, 16 May 2009

January 2010. A snowy new term started, and memories of an eventful year began to fade just as they had in 1910.

The tortoise and the hare on the flag, high on its pole, welcomed everyone back, and so did the new Headmaster, Dr Steve Bailey. Dr Bailey was already familiar with Twyford, for, as well as being a Housemaster at Winchester, he had been a Governor of the School for some years. He holds an international reputation as an historian of sport and the Olympic Games.

So, as this narrative draws to a close, it is time to bid farewell to the first two centuries.

In 1809 the boys who had been taught at Segar's, just off Queen Street in Twyford village, must have felt strange coming to such a fine house for their schooling: however, we should remember that most of their school life would have been spent in rather less salubrious conditions at the rear of the building.

That first century had passed comparatively uneventfully; towards its end, however, the beginnings of the world that we know had begun to stir. The petrol-driven motorised carriage was developed from about 1885; ten years later, just when the first copy of *The Twyfordian* was printed, Marconi succeeded in transmitting basic electrical signals from one end of his house to the other signalling the dawn of radio. Only 14 years later, in 1909, the School held a special day to celebrate 100 years since the move from Segar's.

Thereafter, boys continued their schooling and played their games – only partially disturbed by two catastrophic World Wars. These had been followed by the looming threat of devastating nuclear conflict during what was known as the Cold War between the western democracies and the communist world led by the Soviet Union. Still the lessons had been taught and the matches played. Twyfordians went on their way to their senior schools – and then out into the adult world

Dr Steve Bailey
Headmaster

– in the same way as they always had: with sound foundations for their future lives.

Afterword

Stepping out on a journey is always an exciting time. For a school early in its third century, it is valuable to have a clear understanding of footprints left by those who have passed this way before us. In this book the authors have cast light upon many of these footprints.

Search as I may, I have, so far, found no earth closets, cupboards full of canes or hordes of rampaging earwigs: the pony no longer pulls the mower, and electricity, at last, goes safely round the corners. Twyford is a thoroughly modern school, albeit shaped and strengthened by its long history.

In future years we can expect the scenery to change – buildings come and go – but the ethos will remain: a family school with Christian values that strives to develop in children a lifelong love of learning and a caring outlook.

Education should lead children to believe that they have a responsibility and a capacity to shape the society in which they will live. On the way to their senior schools Twyfordians learn to identify excellence, and to work to achieve the very best they can in a wide range of skills and pursuits. They learn to value differences and to respect each other.

It is my hope that the Twyfordians of today will cherish our heritage and will be able to reflect, in future years, that Twyford first gave them the attributes and confidence with which to build fulfilling lives.

School Photographs 1909 and 2009

Twyford School 1909

In the nineteenth century the pupil roll fluctuated between about 35 and 60. From 1900 the numbers rose to about 70 pupils, although there was a steep drop to 37 in the 1930s. However, by 1980 there were 94 children in the School. In the years since then a major expansion has taken place, not only in facilities but in numbers. A Pre-Prep Department was opened in 1985, the School became co-educational and by 2009 there were 376 children.

In **1909** there were 69 boys in the School, and nine schoolmasters. Boys came to the School at the age of seven or eight years, and usually stayed for five years. The School was divided into the Upper School (the top two years), and the Lower School (the lower three years), and some year groups had two classes. There was not a rigid age division between year groups. In 1909 each of the eight classes had between five and twelve boys.

By **2009**, there were 376 children aged 3-13 years, 62 teaching staff and 23 support staff. The children aged 3-7 are in the Pre-Prep Department where there is a single Nursery class, and two classes in each of Reception, Year 1 and Year 2. The Prep School has three classes in each of six year groups – Year 3 (for children aged 7-8) to Year 8. Each class in the School has about 16 children, athough numbers vary slightly.

Pre-Prep 2009

Main School 2009

These photographs have been reproduced by kind permission of Gillman & Soame photographers and can be re-ordered by visiting www.gsarchive.co.uk or telephoning 01869 328200

117 ✧

Headmasters

Mr Hannington
1793-c1798

Revd L.M. Stretch
c1798-c1811

Revd L. Clarke
c1811-1815

Revd J.G. Bedford
1815-1833

Revd R. Wickham
1834-1848

Revd J.C. Roberts
1849-1854

Revd G.W. Kitchin
1855-1861

Revd L. Wickham
1862-1887

Revd C.T. Wickham
1888-1910*

H.C. McDonell
1910-1937

Revd R.G. Wickham
1937-1963

D.T. Wickham
1963-1983

P.R.D. Gould
1983-1996

P.F. Fawkes
1997-2002

Dr D. Livingstone
2003-2009

Dr S.J. Bailey
2010-

* with H.C. Strahan, Headmaster in Partnership 1890-1896

Governors and Trustees

Since the establishment of the Twyford School Trust in 1955 the School has been served by many able and dedicated people as Trustees, and, in many cases, as Governors at the same time. Coming from a variety of professional backgrounds and skills, it is they who set the general policy of the School. They have been the guardians of the School's ethos and reputation, and most have served for several – sometimes many – years. They have given a great deal of their time, experience, and wise counsel to the School for no recompense other than the satisfaction of seeing Twyford thrive. The Constitution was revised in 2003, and again in 2008, when the role of non-Governor trustees lapsed.

Chairman of Governing Body				Chairman of Trust/Company			
C.D. Scriven	1955 - 1957	A.G.G. Cazalet	1977 - 1985	The Rt. Hon. Lord Tucker	1956 - 1961	A.G.G. Cazalet	1996 - 2002
W.S.C. Tully	1957 - 1964	R.N. Stober	1985 - 1999	The Rt. Hon. Lord Devlin	1961 - 1967	R.N. Stober	2002 - 2003
C.W. Parkinson	1964 - 1970	C.E. Monaghan	1999 - 2006	H.E. Hill	1967 - 1973	C.E. Monaghan	2003 - 2006
M.R.T. Lowth	1970 - 1975	S.P. Kelly	2006 -	G.A. Loveday	1973 - 1978	S.P. Kelly	2006 - 2008
M.O.P. Francis	1975 - 1977			M.R.T. Lowth	1978 - 1996		

Key: C – Chairman G – Governor T – Trustee

Lord Tucker – T 1956-63 (C 1956-61).

C.D. Scriven – G 1955-57 (C 1955-57); T 1956-64.

W.S.C. Tully – G 1955-64 (C 1957-64); T 1956-65.

Admiral Sir William Andrewes – G 1957-68; T 1956-68.

Major J.C. Bull – T 1956-61.

Sir Patrick Devlin (later Lord Devlin) – T 1956-67 (C 1961-67).

G.C.W. Dicker – G 1955-65; T 1956-65.

D.P.M. Hall – T 1956-66.

Dr B.W. Hunt – T 1956-65.

R.A.U. Jennings – T 1956-86.

W.E. Parker – T 1956-64.

C.W. Parkinson – G 1964-70 (C 1964-70); T 1956-70.

H.E. Hill – G 1958-64; T 1957-73 (C 1967-73).

C. Mason – T 1962-95.

Revd R.G. Wickham – T 1963-93; (Life President 1990-93).

C.F. Badcock – G 1965-73; T 1965-76.

Lt Cdr D.E.C. Barratt RN – T 1965-76.

A.D. Donger – T 1965-76.

H.G. Edwards – T 1965-77.

D.B. Huffam – T 1965-72.

M.R.T. Lowth – G 1966-75 (C 1970-75); T 1965-96 (C 1978-96).

J.H. Paterson – G 1978-84; T 1965-02.

S.H.J. Roth – T 1965-73.

R.M.O. Stanley – G 1965-71; T 1965-72.

J.G. Stow – T 1965-76.

J.R. Thompson – T 1965-77.

M.O.P. Francis – G 1970-77 (C 1975-77); T 1969-99.

A.H. Cadell – T 1971-76.

Dr T.R. Maurice – G 1972-79; T 1971-91.

Dr J.A. Whillis – G 1971-78; T 1971-82.

G.A. Loveday – T 1973-78 (C 1973-78).

R.J. Massen – G 1974-82; T 1973-90.

A.G.G. Cazalet – G 1975-85 (C 1977-85); T 1975-02 (C 1996-02).

C.C. Evers – G 1979-95; T 1977-95.

R.N. Stober – G 1980-99 (C 1985-99); T 1977-06 (C 2002-03).

M.P. Birley – T 1978-94.

T. Devlin – G 1996-03; T 1978-85 and 1995-03.

Mrs J.B. Howman – G 1982-00; T 1981-08.

E.A.M. MacAlpine – G 1982-85; T 1981-85.

T.R. Cookson – G 1983-96; T 1982-95.

C.R.J. Eglington – G 1984- ; T 1984-2008.

J.V.C. Russell – T 1985-00.

C.E. Monaghan – G 1986-06 (C 1999-06); T 1986-2008 (C 2003-06).

P.W. Brazier – G 1992- ; T 1991-08.

D. Christie – G 1992-98; T 1991-98.

S.F. Eliot – G 1997-03; T 1991-03.

Dr H.L. Harvey – G 1996-03; T 1995-03.

Cdr A. Higham RN – T 1998-08.

G. Neil-Dwyer – T 1998-03.

Mrs F.E. White – G 2001-2010 ; T 1998-08.

D.T. Wickham – T 1998-05.

Dr S.J. Bailey – G 2001-09; T 2000-08.

Mrs C. Jones – T 2001-05.

S.P. Kelly – G 2001- (C 2006-); T 2001-08 (C 2006-08).

M. Le May – G 2004- ; T 2001-08.

Mrs J.A. Hawkes – G 2007-08; T 2004-08.

Mrs S. Sowden – G 2004-2010 ; T 2004-08.

A.J. Thould – G 2004- ; T 2004-08.

G. Marsh – G 2006-09; T 2006-08.

M.K.C. Wills – G 2006- ; T 2006-08.

Mrs C.E. Chaplin-Rogers – G 2009-

Mrs F. Dunger – G 2009-

P.M.H. Herring – G 2009-

Dr J.E. Hodgins – G 2009-

J.D. Lever – G 2009-

Some Notable Old Twyfordians
Compiled by Andrew Keeling

James Adams
b. 1980
Cricketer. Hampshire Cricket Club 'Player of the Year', 2009.

Adm Sir Edwyn Alexander-Sinclair GCB MVO JP DL
1865-1945
As Commodore, 1st Light Cruiser Squadron, he was first to report the presence of the enemy which triggered the Battle of Jutland. Principal ADC to King George V.

Adm Sir William Andrewes KBE CB DSO
1899-1974
Commander Commonwealth naval forces in Korean War. NATO Deputy Supreme Allied Commander, Atlantic.

Dr Terence Armstrong MA PhD
1920-1996
Director of Scott Polar Research Institute. Awarded Royal Geographical Society's Victoria medal.

Sir Christopher Audland KCMG DL
b. 1926
Deputy Secretary-General, European Commission. Director-General for Energy, European Commission.

Thomas Baring, Earl of Northbrook GCSI PC DCL LLD FRS
1826-1904
Viceroy of India, 1872-1876. First Lord of the Admiralty. Lord-Lieutenant of Hampshire. President of the Royal Geographical Society.

Gen Sir Robert Biddulph GCB GCMG
1835-1918
Director-General, Military Education. Governor of Gibraltar, 1893-1900.

Wilfrid Scawen Blunt
1840-1922
Poet, traveller and writer.

Sir Charles Cavendish Boyle KCMG
1849-1916
Governor of Newfoundland (1901-1904) and Mauritius (1904-1911).

Arthur Gilbert Bradley
1850-1943
Author of books on history and topography, and of several biographies.

Clarence Napier Bruce GBE LLD
Baron Aberdare
1885-1957
Played cricket for Middlesex. Champion Racquets, Real Tennis and Lawn Tennis player. Member of the International Olympic Committee.

Hon Victor Austin Bruce
1897-1978
Racing driver. First Briton to win the Monte Carlo Rally.

'Jock' Bruce-Gardyne MP
Baron Bruce-Gardyne
1930-1990
Conservative politician and journalist. Vice President of the National Deaf Children's Society.

Most Revd Richard Chenevix Trench DD DCL PC
1807-1886
Anglican archbishop and poet. Professor of Theology, King's College London. Dean of Westminster. Archbishop of Dublin.

Adm Arthur Christian CB MVO
1863-1926
Rear Admiral in Eastern Mediterranean. Commanded naval forces at Suvla Bay, and subsequent operations up to and including the evacuation of Gallipoli.

Gen Sir Walter Congreve VC KCB MVO
1862-1927
Won VC at Colenso in 1899. Governor of Malta, 1924-1927.

Euan Stewart Cooper-Willis
b. 1920
Founder, with his wife, Susan Williams-Ellis, of Portmeirion Potteries.

Richard Crossman MP OBE
1907-1974
Health and Social Security Secretary. Famous for his *'Diaries of a Cabinet Minister'*.

Freeman John Dyson FRS
b. 1923
Mathematical Physicist. Made significant contributions to the physics of quantum electrodynamics.

Anthony Eyton RA
b. 1923
Painter. Senior Academician of the Royal Academy.

Very Revd Thomas Garnier
1809-1863
Dean of Lincoln. Rowed for Oxford in first University Boat Race in 1849.

Brig Gen Sir George Gater GCMG KCB Kt DSO(Bar) DipEd
1886-1963
Awe-inspiring Army service in WW1. Senior Local Authority education administrator.

Col Sir Eric Gore-Browne Kt DSO OBE TD
1885-1964
Chairman, Glyn, Mills and Co. Chairman of the Southern Railway.

Basil Gray CB CBE MA FBA
1904-1989
Keeper of Oriental Antiquities, British Museum.

Roderick Haig-Brown LLD
1908-1976
Famous for his writing on fly fishing; expert on trout and the Pacific salmon. Chancellor, University of Victoria.

Maj Gen Sir Henry Hallam-Parr KCB CMG
1847-1914
Colonel, Somerset Light Infantry. ADC to Queen Victoria.

Very Revd Hugh Heywood MA
1896-1987
Dean, Gonville and Caius College, Cambridge. Provost of Southwell.

Thomas Hughes QC
1822-1896
English lawyer, politician and author. Author of *'Tom Brown's Schooldays'*.

Douglas Hurd CH CBE PC
Baron Hurd of Westwell
b. 1930
Politician and novelist. Northern Ireland Secretary, Home Secretary and Foreign Secretary.

Professor Ernest Fraser Jacob MA DPhil FBA FSA FRHistS
1894-1971
Chichele Professor of Modern History, Oxford. Fellow and Librarian of All Souls, Oxford.

Charles Eamer Kempe
1837-1907
'Pre-Raphaelite' stained glass designer.

Sir Denis Laskey KCMG CVO
1916-1987
Ambassador to Romania and Austria.

John Latham
1921-2006
Artist who pioneered conceptual art.

Professor Charles Lock MA DPhil
b. 1955
Professor of English Literature, Copenhagen.

George Loveday TD
1909-1981
Chairman of the Stock Exchange, 1973-1975

Dominic Mahony
b. 1964
Pentathlete. Won bronze medal in Seoul Olympics. Team GB Modern Pentathlon Team Leader.

Charles Mansfield MA
1819-1855
Chemist and traveller. Discovered process for distillation of benzene from coal tar.

Revd Robert Moberly DD
1845-1903
Regius Professor of Pastoral Theology, Oxford.

Robert Moore
b. 1981
England and Great Britain Hockey player.

Maj Gen Sir Robert Neville KCMG CBE RM
1896-1987
ADC to King George VI.
Governor of the Bahamas, 1950-1953.

Desmond Norman CBE CEng FRAeS
1929-2002
Aircraft Designer. Founder of Britten-Norman, Ltd. Designed the Islander and Trilander aircraft.

Sir Edmund Parker Kt CBE
1908-1981
Chairman of Price Waterhouse. President of the Institute of Chartered Accountants.

Rt Hon Sir Jonathan Parker Kt PC
b. 1937
Judge of the High Court of Justice, Chancery Division. Lord Justice of Appeal.

Sir Hubert Parry Bt CVO JP MA MusD DCL LLD
1848-1918
Composer. Director of the Royal College of Music. Professor of Music, Oxford.

Professor Hugh Pelham PhD FRS
b. 1954
Director of the Medical Research Council, Laboratory of Molecular Biology, Cambridge.

Sir Michael Perrin Kt CBE FRSC
1905-1988
Chemist. Created the first practical polythene. Directed the first British atomic bomb programme. Chairman, the Wellcome Foundation, 1953-1970.

Hon Capt Roland Philipps MC
1890-1916
Scout Commissioner for NE London. Wrote several books on Scouting.

Alexander Pope
1688-1744
Renowned English poet and satirist. At the Roman Catholic Twyford School c1696.

John Poynder-Dickson GCMG GBE DSO
Baron Islington
1866-1936
Governor of New Zealand, 1910-1912.

Rt Hon John Rawlinson JP PC KC LLD
1860-1926
Played football for England. Played for Old Etonians in winning FA Cup side. Barrister and MP for Cambridge University.

Alister Robinson
b. 1970
World Doubles Racquets Champion 2005-2007.

Maj Gen Sir Andrew Russell KCB KCMG DSO
1868-1960
Commanded the Anzac Forces at Gallipoli. Commander of the NZ Division. Inspector-General of the Forces in NZ.

Philip Lutley Sclater MA DSc PhD FRS
1829-1913
Lawyer and zoologist. Secretary of the Zoological Society of London for over 40 years.

Rt Rev Roscow George Shedden DD
1882-1956
Bishop of Nassau, 1919-1931.

Evelyn Philip Shirley LLD
1812-1882
Antiquary and genealogist.

Cosby Smallpeice DSc
1896-1977
Engineer, inventor and philanthropist. Founder of the Smallpeice Trust.

Sir Nigel Edward Strutt Kt TD DL
1916-2004
Farmer. Master of the Farmers' Company. President, Royal Agricultural Society.

Raymond Wilson Sturge
1904-1984
Chairman, Lloyd's of London, 1964-1966. President, Insurance Institute of London.

Professor Humphrey Sumner MA FBA FRHistS
1893-1951
Professor of History, Edinburgh. Warden of All Souls, Oxford, 1945-1951.

Christopher Tatham
1924-2006
Wine merchant and broker.
Chairman, Institute of Masters of Wine.

Adm Sir Ernest Troubridge KCMG CB MVO
1862-1926
Chief of War Staff, Admiralty. Commander, Mediterranean Cruiser Squadron. Head of British Naval Mission to Serbia. President of the International Commission of the Danube.

Brian Trubshaw CBE MVO FRAeS
1924-2001
Notable test pilot and the first British pilot to fly Concorde.

Sir Frederick Tucker PC Kt
Baron Tucker
1888-1975
Lord Justice of Appeal, 1950-1961. Presided at trial of William Joyce (Lord Haw Haw).

Sir Mark Tully KBE
b. 1935
India Correspondent and broadcaster, BBC.

Rt Rev Gerald Vernon
1899-1963
Bishop of Madagascar, 1940-1950. Dean of Belize, British Honduras, 1957-1963.

Professor Arthur Verrall LittD
1851-1912
Classical scholar. First King Edward VII Professor of English Literature, Cambridge.

Index

Illustrations in bold

Acknowledgements

We are grateful to the many people who have helped with the production of this book. In particular, we would like to thank our wives, Liz Porteous and Alison Stott, for their unstinting help, encouragement, and forbearance; David Wickham for allowing us to draw freely upon his time and his prodigious memory of Twyford School; Richard Gould for his invigorating company and valuable suggestions; Andrew Keeling for compiling the list of 'Some Notable Old Twyfordians' and for much other help; Angus Stott for his drawings of School features; and our publisher George Mann who has patiently turned our drafts into presentable form.

Will and Shirley Latham of TDS Photographic, Twyford, have cheerfully responded to our many requests for digital images of archive material, and photographers Tiddy Maitland-Titterton and Brynja Maughan lent their professional eyes to help illustrate the book. Of those members of the School staff who have generously tolerated our requests for assistance, Gordon Henderson, John Hudson, Beverley Lambert, Mandy Parker, Penny Unwin and Luke Wordley deserve special mention. For permission to use pictures from their collections, we owe our thanks to Miss H. Best, Daf Herridge, Mrs A. Roberts, and Sue Sullivan (for pictures from the Len Lampard collection).

We are also grateful to the following organisations which kindly supplied and gave us permission to use images: Fotoflite for the image of SS Uganda; Gillman & Soame for the 2009 School photographs; Radley College for the photograph of Desmond Cancellor and other material; the Representative Church Body, Dublin for a copy of the painting of Archbishop Chevenix Trench; the Royal Green Jackets (Rifles) Museum for images of Captain Congreve's portrait and VC; Gillman and Soame for the School Photographs;

and the Watts Gallery, Compton, Guildford for a copy of the painting of Thomas Hughes. Phillimore and Son kindly allowed us to use an extract from 'A Chronicle of Small Beer'.

Of the Old Twyfordians who have shared their memories, our thanks are due particularly to G.M. Audland, T.M. Lawrie and A.R.H. Worssam for permission to include their recollections in the book, and to M.R.T. Lowth for allowing us to print a letter from his ancestor, Charles Lowth.

Many others have willingly given us help in research or procurement of images for which we thank them. They include: Mark Bills, Curator, Watts Gallery; Suzanne Foster, Archivist, Winchester College; Lucy Martin, Scott Polar Research Institute, University of Cambridge; Christine Pullen, Curator, Royal Green Jackets (Rifles) Museum; Raymond Refaussé, Librarian and Archivist, Representative Church Body, Dublin; Clare Sargent, Archivist, Radley College; Edward Wakeling, Editor of *Lewis Carroll's Diaries*.

Bibliography

We are particularly indebted to the two previous historians of the School. The Revd C.T. Wickham wrote *The Story of Twyford School* (1909) to celebrate the centenary of the School in its present home. The Revd R.G. Wickham, in his book *Shades of the Prison House* (1986), painted a picture of the School during much of its second century, as well as including an account of his research into the pre-1745 Roman Catholic Twyford School.

Curtis, G.C.S., *A Chronicle of Small Beer*, (Chichester: Phillimore & Co. Ltd, 1970)

Hughes, T., *Tom Brown's Schooldays*

Leinster-Mackay, D., *The Rise of the English Prep School*, (Lewis, East Sussex: The Falmer Press, 1984)

Pearce, D. and Crooks, S., *Twyford, Ringing the Changes*, (Winchester: George Mann Publications, 1999)

Wickham, C.T., *The Story of Twyford School*, (Winchester: Warren & Son, The Wykeham Press, 1909)

Wickham, R.G., *Shades of the Prison House*, (Winchester: Foxbury Press, 1986)

Wilson, H.W., *With the Flag to Pretoria*, (London: Harmsworth Brothers, 1900)

The Chronicles of the Garniers of Hampshire (1900)

Picture Credits

t - top; b - bottom; l - left; r - right; c - centre; m - middle
All images in this book are taken from the Twyford School archive collection or from the authors' own collections except for those below which are reproduced by kind permission of the following lenders:

Miss H. Best 79tr; Cassini Publishing Ltd 19mr; Fotoflite 87; Gillman & Soame 117, 118bc; Tony & Moira Goodburn 108bm; Daf Herridge 89; Anne Hibberd 101bl; The Trustees of the Imperial War Museum, London 59, 66r; Rose Job 108tl; M.R.T. Lowth l4 cl; Tiddy Maitland-Titterton 2bl,br, 15tc, 100t, 101tr,br,bc; 110ml; 111mc,bc, br; 112 bl,tr; back endpaper (right); Brynja Maughan 25tl, 36, 41b, 44, 45, 63, 67ml,bl,br, 83tc; Newsquest 82, 90br; Claire Porteous 29; Radley College 65; Representative Church Body, Dublin 12ml; Royal Green Jackets (Rifles) Museum 43m, 43r; Mrs A. Roberts 6, 47br; Andrew Sollars 114r, 118br; Scott Polar Research Institute, University of Cambridge 53tr,br; Angus Stott 5, 24, 32tr, 33tl, 47tr, 49tc, 54ml, 95tl, back endpaper (left); Sue Sullivan (from the Len Lampard collection) 62ml, 79bm; V&A Images/Victoria and Albert Museum, London 64; Watts Gallery (picture adopted by Rugby School as part of the 'Adopt a Watts' programme) 17.

Every effort has been made to credit any existing copyright holders for material used in this book. If any have been inadvertently overlooked, they are invited to contact Twyford School.

It's dogged as does it